Crossline to Bhutan

by

Suraj Budathoki

DORRANCE PUBLISHING CO
EST. 1920
PITTSBURGH, PENNSYLVANIA 15238

Dorrance Publishing Co
585 Alpha Drive
Suite 103
Pittsburgh, PA 15238
Visit our website at www.dorrancebookstore.com

ISBN: 979-8-89127-566-9
eISBN: 979-8-89127-064-0

Dedication

I dedicate this book to my parents, with all my heart and soul. You have been the pillars of my life, the ones who have always been there for me, no matter what. You have sacrificed so much for me, and I can never thank you enough. You left your own country just to save our lives and provide us with all the necessities. I cannot even imagine the challenges you must have faced, leaving behind everything you knew and loved, to start afresh in a new and unknown land. Despite all the difficulties, you worked tirelessly in the refugee camps, doing everything in your power to ensure that we had a roof over our heads, food to eat, and clothes to wear. You went to the forest and gathered wild food for us, and even begged in the village just to feed us. My love for you is like a burning flame that had, has, and will never dim. You have always been there to support, encourage, and to push me to achieve my dreams. You have been my inspiration, my role models, and my guiding lights. I owe everything I am and have today to you, my dearest parents. I am grateful beyond measure for the sacrifices you made, the love you have shown me, and the lessons you have taught me.

This book is a testament to your unwavering love and support, and I hope it makes you proud.

With love and gratitude,
Suraj Budathoki

Acknowledgment

I would like to take a moment to express my heartfelt gratitude to my birth country, Bhutan. You made me the person I am today. Your struggles, beauty, and people have all played a vital role in shaping my perspective on life, resilience, and perseverance. My journey as a refugee was not an easy one. It was fraught with challenges, obstacles, and heartbreaks. Yet, I emerged from it stronger, more compassionate, and determined than ever before. I owe this resilience to Bhutan, the country that gave me the strength to overcome every hurdle that came my way.

I also want to acknowledge my wife, who has been my pillar of strength throughout this journey. She provided me with the time and space to write this book. I couldn't have done it without her unfaltering support and love.

Lastly, I want to thank my two children, Brianna and Bastian, for understanding the time I needed to invest in this book. Your love and support kept me going. I am proud to have you as my children.

To Bhutan, my wife, and my children, thank you from the bottom of my heart. Your resolute love and support have made this book possible, and I am forever grateful to have you in my life.

Contents

About the Author

Suraj Budathoki hails from the scenic town of Samrang, nestled between Tibet and India in the beautiful country of Bhutan. With a deep passion for peacebuilding and reconciliation, he aspires to heal the wounds of his homeland and extend his efforts to other parts of the world.

Suraj's educational journey has equipped him with a broad understanding of political science and international relations. He holds a bachelor's degree in Political Science from Southern New Hampshire University and a master's degree in International Relations from Norwich University. Currently, Suraj is pursuing his PhD in Transformative Social Change at Saybrook University, with a focus on creating positive peace in Bhutan and beyond.

As an author and writer, Suraj's experiential knowledge, dedication to his craft, and concern for his fellow men are evident. He has written half a dozen opinion pieces in various newspapers, and his breakthrough memoir, *Crossline to Bhutan*, offers readers a captivating exploration of his personal journey and experiences.

In his leisure time, Suraj finds solace in the pages of nonfiction books and the thought-provoking narratives of documentary films. He dreams of embarking on the breathtaking Tiger's Nest Trail in Paro Dzong, Bhutan, a place that holds a special allure for him.

Suraj's interests extend beyond personal enrichment. He actively engages in voluntary work and is a staunch advocate for peace and social justice. He demonstrates his dedication to these causes through his tireless pursuit of positive change and his desire to reunite families in his homeland. Also, having been a refugee in Nepal for nineteen years (1990–2009), he reads and writes Nepali, understands Hindi, and he is very much interested in not only South Asian politics but international politics as well. Following this passion, he furthered his knowledge and experience of American politics through his involvement with Bernie Sanders's run back in the 2020 presidential elections, and even more so, as the President of Peace Initiative Bhutan (PIB).

As he continues to make a significant impact in the realm of peacebuilding, he is hopeful of visiting his cherished birth country, Bhutan, where he aims to contribute to its healing process. With aspirations to create lasting peace and reconciliation, Suraj's dreams are deeply rooted in his desire to build a better world for generations to come.

Reflecting his commitment to inner peace, Suraj draws inspiration from the words of the Dalai Lama: "Do not let the behavior of others destroy your inner peace." These words serve as a guiding principle in his life and work, fueling his determination to make a positive difference.

Preface

The royal government of Bhutan forcibly expelled its citizens in the late 1980s and early 1990s, and the refugee situation has persisted today, with no or minimal attention from regional and international communities.

The global and regional powers have deserted the issue despite being present for decades and continue abusing human rights, including the right to return, nationality, and identity. This issue has been exacerbated by a need for a blueprint strategy among exiled leaders, internal discord, Bhutan's extrapolative state of nonviolence, and India's and foreign countries' strategic significance of Bhutan in the region. As a result, resolving this crisis has become ever more intricate and challenging.

Bhutan has long presented itself as a nation that prioritizes peace and nonviolence. Their Gross National Happiness policy drastically neutralized its foreign intervention and pushed it to repatriate its citizens from the refugee camps. Despite this image, the country's treatment of refugees has been, in fact, quite turbulent. The political situation in Bhutan has been left unaltered by Western democracies prioritizing their strategic interests in this region, resulting in a lack of response or action to address the needs of Bhutanese refugees. On the other hand, Bhutan profusely utilized its geo-strategic location, with its border shared with China, which has provided the country with a unique position in the region. The Bhutanese government has used this location to its advantage by positioning itself as a valuable ally to India and the Western democracies. Due to this, its foreign allies could not influence or press Bhutan to repatriate its citizens from the refugee camps and ask them to respect and promote human rights, as it should.

The exiled Bhutanese leaders also failed big-time to form a unified front with common strategies, goals, and approaches, leaving the refugees in need of proper guidance, direction, and a clear sense of purpose. This disunity among the leaders has created a leadership vacuum, further exacerbating the situation for the refugees. The lack of effective strategic planning and global solidarity have been a significant obstacle in confronting the crisis, and the reactive tactic of the exiled leaders has amply stalled their ability to make any progress.

The Bhutanese refugee crisis has been compounded by the Indian government's reluctance to resolve the issue, owing to its close alliance and strategic partnership with Bhutan. India's focus on maintaining its strategic interests in Bhutan has taken precedence over addressing the refugee crisis, creating a long-standing problem. Additionally, the Bhutanese government's manipulation of its geopolitical location and portrayal as a buffer state between India and China has enabled it to garner support from Western democracies, despite human rights violations against its citizens.

In recent years, the circumstances of Bhutanese refugees have transformed. Many have been resettled and granted citizenship in different nations, which has altered their requirements. Due to their forced expulsion, they have been disconnected from their families and cannot reunite during important life events such as funerals or illness. Furthermore, many political detainees have received life sentences, and their families are unaware of their health status.

Resettled Bhutanese individuals residing in the United States face mental health issues and elevated rates of suicide due to the traumatic experiences endured during their confinement and forced displacement. Restoration of their connection with their cultural roots through peacebuilding and reconciliation efforts present a promising approach to addressing the ongoing suffering of Bhutanese refugees and promoting stability in the region.

This unfortunate ongoing infliction can be resolved through dialogue, and it is in the best interest of the government of Bhutan. Releasing incarcerated political detainees could alleviate Bhutan's financial burden and improve its relations with other countries. Allowing family unification in Bhutan would increase the happiness of the Bhutanese citizens, decrease the mental health issues of the exiled Bhutanese, and improve the families' financial status in Bhutan. This will improve the people-to-people relationships, and eventually, lead to conflict resolution.

Thus, the time has been long overdue for all the Bhutanese leaders, regional, and international powers to help build sustainable peace and reconciliation in Bhutan. This process will help resolve the ongoing Bhutanese suffering since the 1990s. Acknowledging past wrongs is a critical element in promoting peacebuilding and reconciliation. Addressing the root causes of conflict requires identifying and addressing the underlying social, economic, and political factors that contribute to conflict. Justice is essential for accountability and for promoting fairness and equality.

Eleanor Roosevelt once said, "It is not enough to talk about peace. One must believe in it. And it is not enough to believe in it. One must work at it." It is time to invest ourselves in building sustainable peace and reconciliation in Bhutan. Bhutan deserves positive peace and exiled Bhutanese—healing and dignity.

Chapter 1

Bhutan

We've all seen happy families. Most of us sometimes wish that our families were as happy as those families. However, sometimes we fail to comprehend that the families that seem joyful and complete from the outside can sometimes be broken, miserable, and barely sticking together to create a façade of happiness, unity, and progress. Most people just think, "Well, wow, what a great family and what wide smiles." Just like a family that lives through and for a façade of happiness, my home country, Bhutan, too, lives through a façade.

I took the liberty of calling it my home country because it just so happened that my forefathers, despite having Nepali lineage had proof of documentation of being Bhutanese through some papers. Many, like me, were expelled from the country because the government changed the laws, which made the exiled Bhutanese "illegal" in their own state. People from outside Bhutan always remember the Bhutanese as people who live in unity and have been ranking incredibly high, if not the highest, on the gross national happiness index. On the inside of Bhutan, however, this happiness isn't as glittery as it looks from the outside.

The insiders and the population of Bhutan have always been extremely diverse. There are several ethnic communities with their own set of values, traditions, customs, and ways of living that aren't just beautiful but also colorful and add valor to the land of Bhutan. The different cultural and traditional groups like the Ethnic Nepali like myself, Lhotshampas, and others have merged within the culture, especially with the Northern Bhutanese culture, which also resembles the neighboring Tibetan culture. However, as unfortunate as it might sound, the concept of "Bhutanese" identity has often proved costly for the diversity that remains embedded within Bhutan even today.

Ideally, this would make one big family like many people perceive India to be. However, the problems within India are known only to those within India and the nearby outsiders. In the case of Bhutan, not even the nearby outsiders are aware of the catastrophic citizenship conundrum that haunts many in Bhutan. Even today, there are thousands of ethnic Nepali individuals in Bhutan who, despite their bread and butter in Bhutan, remain stateless despite their forefathers' residence in Bhutan. They are not acknowledged as being Bhutanese.

From their language to their traditions and customs, everything has had to come down to either a halt or completely vanish. This has brutally murdered the diversity and colorful culture that Bhutan once endorsed. The late 1980s saw a climate in Bhutan where the practice of any culture deemed not purely Bhutanese was met with disapproval or outright prohibition. This policy sowed the seeds of discontent among the Ethnic Nepali Bhutanese citizens. Indeed, the situation is gradually evolving today.

Now, who decides what is "Pure Bhutanese" is something that remains subjective and is definitely inclined towards those in power.

On the surface, the banning and eliminating of any diversity is something that is looked at as unison. It is something that is creating unity amongst the people of Bhutan, but as a child who grew up in Bhutan in the nineties, I know it is more than just that. Using division as a form of unity is something that remains absurd. It is rather juxtaposed, if one could argue. As a child going to school in the nineties of Bhutan, I didn't even know cultural differences existed between the families and friends that we interacted with. Everyone was tolerant of the other groups' practices and got themselves involved in the process as well. We knew nothing about politics and just minded our own business.

Isn't that ideally how a diverse country and society should operate? We had friends, a great time, and sometimes we would help each other out in preparing for customs that didn't necessarily belong to our group of beliefs. Everyone was together because we were unaware of our differences, or we wanted peace and acknowledged our differences and learned to live with them. The level of tolerance and the concept of "US vs. THEM" didn't quite exist for anyone who lived around. Things were changing, though. Policies around us were changing, and they were becoming stricter. We didn't face the brunt of these changes because it is important to understand that the time it takes for a policy to be introduced and then for it to be implemented is the time that we are bound to see a change in the social and cultural fabric.

There was a policy shift in 1985 that turned things around for Bhutan, particularly for those belonging to diversified ethnicities. The National Integration Policy aimed to make Bhutan a single cultural society with everyone following a uniform culture and a tradition that was central to everyone. It no longer left any room for any other culture to be represented, let alone flourish and grow. It became integral to follow Buddhist principles because that is what the "pure Bhutanese" would follow. Other languages, including the extremely widely spoken Nepali, were banned from schools, offices, and any official proceedings. This was appalling, to say the least.

There were apprehensions that existed prior to this. A certain group and set of people were threatened by the growth of different ethnicities and cultures. For example, in 1958, Bhutan introduced a Citizenship Act directed towards Bhutanese whose grandparents or great-grandparents were settlers. That law was known as the Nationality Act of Bhutan.

Those laws appear to be liberal and give citizenship rights to Bhutanse citizens of Nepali origin, but the subsequent Acts made it almost impossible for many Bhutanese of Nepali descent to prove their nationality and commitment to Bhutan, as they had to show their land tax receipt. Many people had birth certificates, but the majority were not provided with the land tax receipt as proof of nationality during the 1988 census time. As a result, they were required to leave Bhutan within the span of 10–15 days, and it was downright horrific to see the implementation of this act.

By that time, ethnic communities were stronger than they were in the '50s, and the backlash on the two policies combined was directed towards the government. This included the Lhotshampas, who were angry, enraged, and just incredibly miserable with the state and position they were threatened to be in. Their rights to citizenship were stripped off in minutes, and years of their dedication and settling into Bhutan were completely disregarded. Later, when I got the chance to speak to leaders and ex-leaders of the time in Bhutan, it was revealed to me that the goal for the king was to depopulate and eventually eliminate the ethnic Nepali from Bhutan.

An example of my conversation with Lhotshampa leader, Teknath Rizal, is in front of us. He was the royal advisor of His Majesty, who told me that the king summoned him to his Royal Palace and asked for suggestions to evict Lhotshampas. According to him, the king was looking for areas to kick out the population that could threaten the majority of the population in Bhutan.

However, many people do not blame His majesty for the chaos. According to the Association of Human Rights Activists, Bhutan, the king was eighteen years old and barely had any knowledge of politics. He was dependent on the people around him for the decision-making process, and they ruined the system, and His Majesty was not diplomatic or experienced enough to handle the situation. Many others have the same thinking, but there are others who opine that he let it continue and never bothered to bring measures to address the issue.

Yet, the king succeeded to a certain extent as well by policy and integration being his cover. There was propaganda that called for unity and a sense of unison within Bhutan, but this unison was coming at the cost of the diversity and vibrance that Bhutan once offered. The vibrance came with many different traditions operating side by side, particularly from the Ethnic Nepali, the Lhotshampas. The conflict had divided the country more than it could unite it, and that is what we will discuss throughout the course of this book.

Chapter 2

Lhotshampas

"Ancient boundaries are meaningless, except for political purposes; old divisions of clan and tribe are sentimental remnants of the pre-atomic age; neither creed nor colour nor place of origin is relevant to the realities of modern power to utterly seek and destroy."

Sydney J. Harris, The Best of Sydney J. Harris

Boundaries. They are created by man, exploited by man, and then also blamed by man. The same can be said about the thin boundary between Nepal and Bhutan. The unique identity and culture of the two states were rooted in threat and fear, due to which one community suffered: Lhotshampas.

The question comes down to this: *who are the Lhotshampas?* In a nutshell, if one was to describe them, these were the people who lived in the Southern region of Bhutan. Their descent or grandparents or great-grandparents brought in from Nepal for agricultural activities in their forest-dense South. The subsequent kings welcomed Nepali from

Nepal with their express interests. They lived there and prospered in their work and personal lives. Therefore, many had five or more generations who lived there happily. Many people like me had grandparents born there in Bhutan because their grandparents or great-grandparents migrated to Bhutan.

The King of Bhutan's official directive was to bring these people and their families in to boost economic engagement in the country at the behest and promise of citizenship. This is a rather sugar-coated and eased-out explanation of who these people have been, but deeper angles are to be explored here. The truth is that Lhotshampas have been in Bhutan since the 1600s. Furthermore, historical accounts reveal that Tsongtsen Gampo, the king of Tibet, undertook the construction of significant landmarks following his marriage to the Nepali Princess Bhrikuti Devi. Notably, he commissioned the creation of Jambay Lhakhang in Bumthang and Kichu Lhakhang in Paro. To achieve these architectural feats, Tsongtsen Gampo enlisted the expertise of skilled Newari craftsmen from Nepal, who brought their exceptional craftsmanship to the projects. Legends have that these craftsmen of the areas chose to make their homes there after completing their remarkable work. It is said that these craftsmen lived there after their work. These narratives are often shared in local legends, historical accounts, and oral traditions.

My own family came to Bhutan with my great-grandfather in the late 1800. Then my grandfather was born in Bhutan in the early 1930s. Where the South was populated with selected families to boost economic activities in the country, the North of Bhutan was the absolute elite. This, to a certain extent, still remains the case. The South was barren, and the North was plush with a tinge of pride. Where the South paid taxes in cash, the North paid in crops and goods to the government. The initial financial disparity between the two opposing ends of the country became one of the reasons behind the eventual clash.

The immigrants from Nepal were regulars until the 1958 Citizenship Act, and then things just turned around like the Ethnic Nepali were uninvited guests to a royal party. Even though they lived there for decades and had families with their children born in Bhutan and had citizenship. However, during the 1990s clash, the children of those immigrants had to leave their country.

Let's get into the details of how that happened and how, unfortunately, despite the humanitarian crises of the Lhotshampas, Bhutan has managed to contain its soft image. Whenever we think of refugees or a humanitarian crisis, what do we think of? Afghanistan? Syria? Yemen? No one ever thinks of Bhutan, do they? Let's think of Bhutan here. Bhutan is regularly described as a place known for never-ending satisfaction and happiness, a nation where traffic signals are viewed as excessively unoriginal. They measure their nation's result by the famous and allegedly groundbreaking Gross National Happiness record. Staying untainted by mass, the travel industry, and governed by a well-known youthful ruler, Bhutan is frequently depicted as a legendary spot, and references to Shangri-La are so overused that they have become dull. Bhutan regularly bests the rundown of the most joyful places to live and is a model of happiness in a hyper-promoted world.

However, if you were to explain Bhutan like this to anyone except the "UNIFORM" Bhutanese, they would undoubtedly beg to differ. It is almost as if a family is pretending to be picture-perfect, but inside the house's walls, only the family members know the actual situation entangled in abuse, violation, and blatant discrimination. Just like a dysfunctional family pretending to be completely normal, Bhutan conceals an exceptionally dim history with an effort that has taken a while.

Most people are unaware of the fact that Bhutan is the world's most significant contributor to refugees per capita. During the 1990s, the nation ousted the Lhotshampa. To elaborate further and reiterate their identity, the Lhotshampas, like me, are an ethnic group with footprints drenched in Bhutanese soil, which make up one-sixth of Bhutan's populace. The ousting remains one of the most aggressive ones in the region and beyond. The Citizenship Act used for the ousting has also been used as a landmark for ethnic oustings by other countries like India in 2019.

Over twenty years, thousands stayed in camps in Nepal, lost in their own country. This is an apparent difference with the unspoiled and plain picture Bhutan has cautiously organized for itself. As the world looks at Syria and the developing refugee emergency in the Mediterranean and concern develops, Bhutan draws in little consideration.

While Bhutan ousted "immigrant workers" during the 1990s, to comprehend the total picture, we need to turn around to the seventh century when Newar craftsmen were brought to build monuments and started living in Bhutan as their citizens since then. The example of Kyichu Lhakhang in Paro and Jombe Lakhang in Bumthang are the monuments that were built during the period of Tibetan Emperor Songtsen Gampo by those craftsmen.

Later in history, they inhabited the place the most during the 1600s Zamdrung Nawang Nyamgel brought in Nepali families to his state with an agreement that increased their population to a greater extent in Bhutan. They have been there from that point forward. Getting comfortable in southern Bhutan, the nation's significant food-delivering six southern districts, their numbers thrived and kept on doing as such for an extensive stretch. They acquired the name Lhotshampa because of their being inhabited in the South. Similarly, people living in Paro are called Paropa.

The removal and ousting of the Lhotshampas didn't occur all of a sudden. Bhutan's Citizenship Acts of 1977 and 1985 joined in exacerbating the situation for the entire ethnic group.

Prior to 1958, there was no concept of citizenship; anyone could live in the state; any people were living there for centuries that had turned them into citizens because of the number of years they lived there. In 1958, the enactment of Citizenship Act granted citizenship to everyone.

In 1988 an enumeration was directed; in any case, ineffectively prepared registration authorities committed various errors in administrating the statistics, just as stirring up ethnic strains. Following the calculation, the Bhutanese government, comprised of Drukpa, understood the degree of the Bhutanese-Nepalese populace living in Bhutan, most outstandingly the Nepali-speaking Lhotshampas ethnic group. Therefore, they made policies with the motive of evicting ethnic Nepalese. Thus, it was more like a war between the government and Lhotshampas.

In the late 1980s and early 1990s, more than 100,000 Lhotshampa left Bhutan, with many professing to have been constrained by the Bhutanese Government. Many were blamed for being expatriates and guaranteed they had confronted savagery and ethnic segregation. Now and then, conflicts between the Bhutan People's Party, overwhelmed by the Lhotshampa, and the public authority are additionally standard.

Following the enumeration, the Bhutanese Government assessed that 28% of the populace were of Nepalese descent. Nonetheless, informal cases orbited that up to 40 percent of the people were Nepalese; this would be viewed as a more significant part of Bhutan. This figure, before too long, acquired a foothold in the public eye and mind. With events paving the way to Sikkim's joining India in 1975 still new in the personalities of Bhutanese pioneers, the move must be made.

Anyway, the populace numbers cited may have been off track with an open line, short work, and the topographical difficulties of directing an evaluation in distant regions. A few assessments put the quantities of the Nepalese populace at just 15%. Before the mass oustings, the Bhutanese Government didn't even attempt a favorable political climate.

Under the "One Nation, One People" strategy, the public authority put social and semantic limitations upon the Lhotshampa, from supplanting Nepalese as a study hall language with Dzongkha to compelling all residents to follow the general clothing standard of the Driglam Namzha. Nepalese normally loathed being obligated to wear the dress of the Ngalop rather than their conventional dress.

Other insincere strategies were utilized by the public authority to control or mutilate populace levels; as per the report of The Diplomat[1], the public administration constrained many ousted individuals, practically all, to sign the deliberate relocation structure before leaving the country. They snatched their identity cards to minimize their chances of returning to the state. These activities have made it difficult for individuals to get back to Bhutan. Segregation and Kafkaesque principles have been conveyed, making life significantly more challenging for the Lhotshampa.

Furthermore, the Diplomat report notes that Nepali-speaking individuals in southern regions needed to create their archives to demonstrate they were in Bhutan before 1958… Bhutanese from different spots are viewed as Bhutan[ese] by [virtue of] their race. This is a glaringly oppressive government strategy. This led to many refugees, and in complete honesty, the number will only rise until the atrocities don't overshadow Bhutan's positive and peace-oriented image.

The absence of a need to keep moving has driven outcasts to mope in camps for quite a long time. There are two functional Bhutanese exile camps in Nepal, down from the first seven. The excess centers have a common populace of approximately 7000, currently. Conditions inside the camps are challenging, as they were never intended to be a super durable arrangement. As this is anything but a significant problem for one or the other, Nepal and Bhutan, with the two sides inclining

---

[1] The Diplomat. (2016, September 21). Bhutan's Dark Secret: The Lhotshampa Expulsion. https://thediplomat.com/2016/09/bhutans-dark-secret-the-lhotshampa-expulsion/

toward recovery in nonpartisan third nations, but are not getting any assistance from other countries.

Bhutan is presently opening up and expanding itself onto the world stage, as shown by the visit of the British Prince William in mid-2016. With Bhutan beginning to make dynamic strides on the world stage, King Jigme Khesar Namgyel Wangchuck ought to be compelled to recognize the separation and inevitable ejection of thousands of Lhotshampas, and so have the ones who followed. The problem is widespread, but the mention of it is not. One primary reason is that Bhutan, a one-man show, is heavily curated and controlled regarding incoming and outgoing information. The people who live in Bhutan know what segregation is like, and they understand the differences. It is not the people of Bhutan but the governments from the past and the government of today that have been targeting the Lhotshampas.

The differences between the two ethnic groups go from religious to cultural. Bhutan has many cultural practices coming in from Tibetan culture, be it the language, the dress codes, or anything else. The ruling class of Bhutan has always been Tibetan in their background, and it becomes incredibly ironic when they want to oust Lhotshampas just because they have a Nepalese background. Where the North was dwelling in the Tibetan culture and Buddhism as their prime religion, the South was focused on Hinduism as their practicing religion. The stark difference in religious ideas and ways became a critical factor in determining that the Lhotshampas were not Bhutanese enough. This still remains the case.

However, every nation somehow survives with diversity. Some of the most prosperous countries in the region and the world have thrived just as well with diversity, and the likes of India are a brilliant example of that over the years. However, the problem became something else. The problem became the fact that the Lhotshampas were progressing economically and climbing up the social ladder. This meant that the wide gap between the North and the South was starting to blur, which remained unacceptable to the North and the ruling class. This divide is what keeps them going.

The Ethnic Nepalese were and still are hugely influenced by Indian culture and politics. They would move to India for higher education as well as work experience. This would groom them, and when they'd come back to Bhutan for work, they wouldn't just occupy some of the best working positions but also end up having some of the most significant political positions. This created a concern for the status quo, and it needed to be addressed as soon as possible. It started with non-appreciation at first and then led to an outright campaign of discriminating, ousting, and segregating a progressive and innocent ethnic group of the nation.

Chapter 3

Bhutan and Threat

It should be noted that Lhotshampas have to provide free labor to construct roads and monasteries in Bhutan. My mother and father participated in this free labor to develop many of these institutions that stand. My father mentioned that he committed to about three to four months of this endless free labor to build Bhutan's infrastructure. However, the Bhutanese Government has a different outlook on the Lhotshampas.

They saw the community as being too closely tied with India and Nepal culturally and linguistically. Besides, the government thought that they should be treated as a labor worker because that's how they came there. The government and many National government officials made it clear that every initiative they took was for the survival of the Ngalop people, who comprised 11 percent of the nation in the 1990s. They were the majority with Sharshops that were akin to their culture and dress code. They feared being overwhelmed demographically by the Lhotshampa minority or any group of Nepali origin.

While the Lhotshampas were at no fault for being treated like absolute strangers, Bhutan as a state has had its reasoning to do what they have been doing, the Bhutan government then and now, has been fearing threats in the face of the Lhotshampas. Be it the language, the traditions, the culture, or anything that Lhotshampas practice, it wasn't exactly aligned with the culture and traditions of Bhutan. This threat led to the imposition of Drukpa culture on the Lhotshampas as an aggressive move to counter a subculture to become the primary culture of Bhutan. From a Lhotshampas perspective, that might be an unfair thing to do, but it makes a tad bit of sense from a Bhutanese perspective. It is, after all, the responsibility of the state to ensure that the culture and traditions of the land remain unharmed. Yet they are required to create a respectful environment to preserve all cultures, not just one.

Even though the imposition went as far as sermons coming up to convert Hindu Lhotshampas to Buddhists, it can be said that the idea of protecting the diverse culture of Bhutan was all right, but the execution of one culture over another was extreme and created chaos for the Lhotshampas. The goal was uniformity with one religion, one culture, language, and even dress code. This is where the national integration policies were aggressively introduced and forcefully assimilated. Let's recap the events in the form of culture and traditions that were detrimental to the Bhutanese traditions.

The Lhotshampas coincided calmly with other ethnic gatherings in Bhutan until the mid-1980s when Bhutan's king and the ruling Druk larger part became stressed that the developing Lhotshampas populace could compromise the greater part position and the traditional Buddhist culture of the Drukpa Bhutanese. The public authority consequently started a mission known as "One Country, One People," or "Bhutanization," to solidify the Bhutanese national identity. The approaches forced the Drukpa clothing regulation, strict practices, and language use on all Bhutanese paying little heed to earlier practices.

These progressions contrarily affected the Lhotshampas people since they didn't wear a similar traditional dress, practice a similar religion, or communicate in a similar language as the northern Bhutanese. The utilization of the Nepali language was precluded in schools, numerous Lhotshampas instructors were excused, and reading material was scorched.

The aim of starting reforms was to encourage integration between the north and south of Bhutan, but with time, that changed as well.

The reforms of the 1950s can be explained in terms of the personality of King Jigme Dorji Wangchuck and Bhutan's relationship with the newly independent India. After the establishment of the monarchy, innovations in Bhutan included a land reform movement (1952) and the creation of the National Assembly (Tshogdu) in 1953. The Nationality Law of Bhutan (1958) was repeatedly used to grant citizenship to the population of southern Bhutan. Schools in southern Bhutan taught Dzongkha as well as Nepali. It was also true that the Lhotshampa contributed to the building of roads and how they were allowed to settle in the previously forbidden southeastern districts of the country.

Nepali-speaking Bhutanese are now living in refugee camps in Nepal with few Drukpas. The number has eventually gone down, but the damage done was severe. Because of the illogical threats the government felt from Nepalese, it resulted in the ethnic cleansing, which ruined Lhotshampas, a lot who just wanted to live there and help the country progress.

By the last part of the 1980s and early 1990s, an emergency had been created. Common liberties infringement, including confinement, detainment before trial, and torment, were not rare. Furthermore, severe and unreasonable prerequisites for demonstrating citizenship were forced on the Lhotshampa people, the majority of whom were denied acknowledgment of their citizenship in any event when they had the option to give documentation. Before the end of 1992, a larger number than 100,000 Lhotshampas had escaped or been constrained out of the country, for the most part into exile camps in Nepal, where many stay right up until today.

There was international involvement as well. The joined pressure of bombed reciprocal discussions among Bhutan and Nepal, almost twenty years of life in the displaced person camps, and destitution made a critical struggle between those Lhotshampas who needed to move to the USA or another Western nation and the people who felt that tolerant resettlement was identical to tolerating rout and would make them less ready to advocate for the right of return to their nation of beginning.

The struggle and conflict remain today, and where from a Lhotshampa perspective, the reason behind that would be hate, lack of tolerance, and sheer authoritarian nature of the Bhutanese Government; from a Bhutanese perspective, the reason would be the protection of the culture, traditions as well as the religion of Bhutan. It was for the survival of the ruling elite, the northern Bhutanese, along with securing national integrity and security, that these policies were enforced upon the citizens. To date, the situation and its reasoning change depending on what lens it is seen with. For the Bhutanese and their ruling elite, it is nationalist and protective. For the Lhotshampas and many outsiders, it is ultra-nationalist and unfair.

Till the 1980s, owing to better education opportunities in India and otherwise, along with better exposure and skill set, the Lhotshampas had gained significant power through the government positions and economic cycle of the country. More so, they were populated in the South, which was where most production for Bhutan was done. They had resources in hand, coupled with skill and education. For Bhutan to consider them a threat may well be justified. The Lhotshampas were also politically conscious along with having ties in neighboring countries, so there was a possibility that the Bhutan government or the king might be inclined to think that the Lhotshampas could be used for anti-national purposes by other nations to destabilize Bhutan.

In a way, the prominence of the Lhotshampas in the economic as well as political arena became a weakling in terms of protection, sovereignty, and safety of Bhutan. It was upon the government to make sure that the country was kept safe and that no neighboring nation could take advantage of the growing ethnic prominence in Bhutan. This prominence had been growing over time, and that alarmed the Bhutanese Government more than ever. Since the 1980s, the Bhutanese Government has argued that illegal immigration threatens to transform the ethnic Bhutanese into a minority group within their own country. A final nail in the coffin came with the power play of demographics in 1989, in which the national census indicated that the Lhotshampas would eventually comprise Bhutan's majority population.

There had also been a lot going on in the region, which effectively strengthened the Bhutanese fear of being overpowered by the Lhotshampas. The Lhotshampas follow Sanatan Hinduism, a prevalent religion in neighboring India and Nepal. The Lhotshampas are culturally different from those who reside in proximity to them in their own country, to the point where they have more in common with fellow Nepalis than they do with local neighboring groups; the Lhotshampas follow Hinduism and speak the Nepali language—two markers of identity similar in Nepal but different in Bhutan—and something that Bhutanese politicians argue adds to the Lhotshampas' sense of "foreignness."

Foreignness has always been problematic for Bhutan. Bhutan—sandwiched between regional giants China and India—has long resisted outside influences, with televisions only allowed in 1999. Its fight against Westernization is often seen as a source of its mystic draw, along with its pursuit of "gross national happiness"— made official policy in 1998—over economic gains.

Following the brutal situation that developed in Bhutan because of the Chinese control of Tibet in 1959 and India's addition of Sikkim in 1975, Bhutan's citizenship laws—which are innately founded on a regional approach—embraced a more prohibitive, ethnocentric tone. Bypassing them, the new king—Jigme Singye Wangchuck—multiplied the residency prerequisites for those functioning the land and significantly increased them for those serving in the Bhutanese Government. The Citizenship Act additionally filled in as an exclusionary strategy with its choice to deny citizenship to people identified with any individual associated with "hostile to public" exercises against Bhutan, its kin, and its lord, eventually preparing for the unequivocal minimization of the last option disagreeing voices—most of whom were individuals from the Nepali-speaking minority.

The threat was taken as seriously as making changes in regard to elections and political forming as well. The 2008 elections were the most crucial in this regard. There was a swap from absolute monarchy for constructional monarchy in the 2008 elections, and it continued to describe the Lhotshampas as immigrants, justifying its nationalistic laws as essential for cultural identity and political stability, according to Freedom House, a think tank.

There have been political parties in the past that have encouraged resistance to this alienation. Such political parties are now banned under the constitution, which states that all parties have to promote national unity and are barred from using ethnicity or religion to attract voters. Parties also have to field candidates in all forty-seven constituencies.

The rules have created a monolithic political environment leaving little room for minority rights, effectively disenfranchising the Lhotshampas who remain in Bhutan from the electoral process. It is unclear how many of the community are still in Bhutan: a 2017 census did not include questions about ethnicity, language, or religion, which would have given an indication of how many people identify as part of the Nepali-speaking, mostly Hindu minority.

The government has prevented human rights groups established by Nepali-speakers from operating, categorizing them as political organizations that do not promote national unity, according to the U.S. State Department. In the lead-up to the 2008 and 2013 polls, there were reports of small protests by Nepali-speakers unable to vote, and during the 2013 elections, international monitors also documented Nepali speakers being turned away from polling centers.[2]

The struggle continues, but both parties have their reasons to remain kaput on their narratives. It will be rather fitting to say here it is truly a matter of perspective, but the fact remains that thousands have lost homes, loved ones, and everything that they call theirs in the process.

---

[2] "Bhutan's Not-so-Happy Evicted Minority, the Lhotshampa." *Yahoo! News*, Yahoo!, https://ph.news.yahoo.com/bhutans-not-happy-evicted-minority-lhotshampa-050813828.html?guccounter=1&guce_referrer=aHR0cHM6Ly93d3cuZ29vZ2xlLmNvbS8&g uce_referrer_sig=AQAAAE3PcN8IiPGiPCaBR7atfbFaXFVNIwWr1fDa8uGqaJRU5ONNeu2IZ2 sCJGnDASvM4arDinyhmyFU9PMQx4qEYa_Cn5wXPraPjh6ZzeVWbPb-qphBp-VAnEJyCyIn6TzY72KtvIUoAyMZfRsWzMLGCxpdRLN7QKXUd8FWAXlXaSrk.

Chapter 4

Country's Monarchy

To understand the Bhutanese government, we need to go back to 1907, when the Bhutanese monarchy started. The Nepalese (Nepali-speaking Bhutanese citizens) were present to support, inaugurate and welcome the first king. It is inaccurate to suggest that the Nepali migrations occurred in the 1950s or later when in fact, the Nepali, or rather Lhotshampas, were present way back in the seventh century.

Therefore, they were present when the first king was inaugurated in Bhutan in 1907. Essentially speaking, Lhotshampas continued to support all Bhutanese kings who assumed the throne.

I have a letter from the Southern Hindus who welcomed King Jigme Singye Wangchuk, the same king who expelled the Lhotshampas. In one paragraph, they wrote,

> *"Oh, King! we look upon thee as the embodiment of power of God of Wealth, wind and fire. We look upon thee as God incarnate on earth for the protection of all the creatures."*

So, the Hindu Lhotshampas viewed every king as a form of God, including King Jigme when he was inaugurated. There were no negative reactions whatsoever toward him when he inherited the throne. There were many Lhotshampa advisors around the king to facilitate his democratic reforms. But this exacerbated tensions with the Ngalop, who believed they were underrepresented in the same governmental institutions as the Parliament.

The king himself ended up doing something very unprecedented. He granted the majority of his powers to the Parliament. There was a provision that if two-thirds of the Parliament voted against the king, the king would be ousted. This provision long ago was implemented by the former king, Jigme's father. Later, Jigme consolidated his power in Bhutan and felt secure that no one would go against him, as he threatened people that people would be banished if they went against him. After that, he included this provision in the current constitution.

There was a growing fear that if the Lhotshampas kept growing in terms of their population, they would gain more members in Parliament and ultimately usurp his authority and the country altogether. I can't say this as a fact, but I believe this is precisely what led to his depopulation methods against the Nepalese minority.

To expand on the transition of the Bhutanese government, I will expound on the period of the seventeenth century in the country. The role of Shabdrung Ngawang Namgyel is relevant in this transition. He was a reincarnated lama and civil administrator. Back then, Bhutan was not the Bhutan of today. It was a region of small, divided states called Penlops. Namgyel ultimately fought with the other small states and conquered them to form a single unified new nation-state of Bhutan.

This is not hearsay; it is documented in many books by credible historians. This story is unverified; however, in popular culture, Shabdrung Ngawang Namgyel went to Nepal, which was not the Nepal of today. It was a divided community of states then. He went to Gorkha and met with the King of Gorkha. He managed to convince the King of Gorkha to bring about forty or fifty Nepalese families to the new state of Bhutan as construction workers. Many of these families settled in Bhutan and participated in creating Bhutan's monasteries, roads and other infrastructure. This is where Nepalese began to form a community in Bhutan instead of the mid-twentieth century.

The government in Bhutan realized that the Lhotshampas of the country had close ties with the people of Nepal and India. The Ngalop did not have this type of connection with their ethnic and cultural brethren like the Tibetans because they resided in the north of Bhutan. Due to having lack of transportation modes, people could not travel there, which contributed to their reduced connection with Tibetans. The Bhutanese government had suspicions about the Lhotshampa community that they were more loyal to the interests of Nepal or India as opposed to Bhutan.

When the East India Company colonized India (EIC), both Bhutan and the EIC engaged in war; Bhutan ultimately surrendered and signed a Treaty with the EIC called the Sinchula Treaty. That Treaty did away with Bhutan's foreign policy and internal security. After India gained its independence, it continued to uphold this Treaty to influence Bhutan. Even when this Treaty was ratified in 2007, Bhutan's foreign and internal policies were guided by India.

India initiated a five-year plan in Bhutan as a means to invest in building Bhutan's infrastructure and electricity projects in the 1960s. But Bhutan did not have enough labor to construct these projects. The Nepali who came as laborers to participate and settle in Bhutan during the '60s were sent back as the projects were completed. Immigration from the South was halted after the implementation of the 1958 citizenship Act. Later, the census was conducted by the government of Bhutan in 1988, and it was found that around 18,000 Lhotshampas were illegally staying in Bhutan (Dhakal, 2022). Dhakal further states in his book that the king assured to address this on a case-by-case basis. Currently, the question is why more than 100,000 Bhutanese were exiled when the census found only 18000 illegal migrants.

My family did their part in the construction of Bhutan's infrastructure. Bhutan today has deployed its army on the Northern side of Bhutan for its national security because both China and India are fighting for influence in Bhutan, and the latter has assumed Bhutan's territorial security. It even placed its army in Northern Bhutan.

The census of 1988 was established to specifically target the Lhotshampa minority in six districts in Southern Bhutan. So, discrimination was rife. The Royal advisory councilor Tek Nath Rizal sent the king a letter stating that the government arbitrarily turned Lhotshampa citizens into non-citizens. He appealed to the king for action, but the king received it as a form of treason. Tek Nath was imprisoned and tortured for about ten years in Chamgang Jail until he was released into exile and spent most of his life in Nepal.

I often speak to him, who admitted to me that the king had previously taken Tek Nath into confidence prior to the census, asking him how they could depopulate Lhotshampa from Bhutan. King Jigme Singye Wangchuk attempted to follow a firm integration policy, like enforcing dress codes and other cultural changes like languages that upset the Lhotshampa minority. This exacerbated the conflict between the Lhotshampa and the government.

I believe that Bhutan could not communicate its policies to the Lhotshampa (or bring Lhotshampas into confidence) or the ethnic Nepalese in the South well. In the same manner, I believe that the Lhotshampa failed to understand national integration's importance in the bigger picture. This understanding would have brought some common ground between the Bhutanese government and the Nepalese minority.

The king is seen in a positive light in Nepal and in the eyes of exiled Bhutanese. He is loved in Bhutan as he is a Western-educated man who has brought new reforms. The Lhotshampa minority sees him as the conduit that can solve the Lhotshampas minority problem. Incidentally, he was born in Nepal. His father was the one who perpetrated the expulsion policy. But we believe that the incumbent king had nothing to do with that policy. This is why I think he may rectify some of the mistakes that occurred in the previous decades.

However, some skeptics believe that the current king is nothing more than a puppet who his father behind the scenes is influencing. But I remain optimistic about the current king and think he may have a different standpoint regarding the issue.

I also want to add that in 1984 and 1989, the Prime Minister of India, Rajiv Gandhi, visited Bhutan many times. People don't know the content of the meetings and what was discussed. I can attest to that. But it is widely speculated that the meeting was about the situation of the Lhotshampa population. After these meetings, the census took place, and the conflicts unraveled. While this is a matter of speculation, it is generally suspected that the Indian Bhutanese meetings had something to do with the changes.

Currently, Bhutan is an independent country. India does not want to lose its influence on Bhutan to China, so it is one of the major donors to the country. Apart from the scholarships provided to Bhutanese students in India, there is a law (policy) where the Bhutanese can buy land and hold jobs in India equally as Indian citizens.

Basically, if I were a Bhutanese citizen, I would reside in India and live there permanently. I could access Indian jobs the same way as any ordinary Indian citizen. However, this privilege is not provided to Indians in the case of Bhutan.

Chapter 5

Culture

As discussed earlier and throughout the course of the book, the rising ethnic Nepalese population in the south of Bhutan became troublesome. This experience of the Bhutanese made them realize the importance of their culture. This was the culture that they stood for and the culture that they endorsed.

Language, amongst many other things, became the point of contestation for the people of Bhutan. It is imperative to talk about language and culture together. They're both interdependent and rather reflect on each other. It could be for better or for worse, but the two are often used interchangeably in verbal communication and legislative changes.

This was when Bhutan's National Identity Project began, which focused on the ideology of *"one nation, one people."* One of the primary and most important aspects of this project was to discuss their motive to bring and promote the actual Bhutanese culture, or rather, what they considered to be actual Bhutanese culture. An integral part of this was the Driglam Namzha.

There is a stringent way of living that governs the lives of the Bhutanese. This way of living under a specific code of conduct is known as Driglam Namzha. Driglam Namzha wasn't always something that existed in Bhutan but was brought in Bhutan by the founding father, Zhabdrung Ngawang Namgyel, who was a Lama and military pioneer from Tibet who looked to bind together Bhutan on the political as well as the social front. There is no arrangement of composing guidelines about the Driglam Namzha. However, it has been a part of normal Bhutanese behavior since the days of yore and has continued through the ages. It has a significant influence on religion, as well as on the day-to-day routines of laymen. This framework is a normal routine and is stringently followed in the country.

Drug (སྒྲུག) stands for stability and conformity, have always been key components for the Bhutanese. As a result, Driglam refers to maintaining a sense of stability while conforming to ideas that further lead to this stability. Yamaha, on the other hand, talks about a system. If brought together and looked at in totality, Driglam Namzha talks about a system of standardized yet cultural values. The system that they introduced with Bhutan also involved the Zacha Dorsum (བཟའ་བཅའ་འགྲོ་གསུམ), which basically refers to the physicality of things, be it through mannerisms, or even something as basic as the kind of walk.

Great peculiarities in Bhutan are characterized by the Buddhist morals of behaviors that include mental, physical, and verbal behaviors. In this unique situation, the idea of Driglam, as Beyzha (direct) or Jaluchalu (moral etiquette), from a free perspective, alludes to great habits which are taken on by the people and intensely affected by the idea of acceptable Buddhist traditional ways of living.

1. Fundamental Rules Of Driglam Namzha

Driglam can be sorted into three disciplines. These include the disciples of verbality, physicality, and mental and psychological ways. Mr. Kunzang Dorji, an exploration official of the Royal Academy of Performing Arts (RAPA), gave an overview of the fundamental rules of Driglam Namzha. He was with RAPA for quite a long time, and he did his certificate and bosses from the College of Language and Culture Studies in Trongsa.

- **Physicality – Attire and Act**

  Physical discipline incorporates the manner in which individuals act and wear garments. The way the Bhutanese eat, act, and walk is also essential for this discipline, known as zhacha dro sum. Outer practices ought to reflect healthy qualities, such as lowliness, restraint, quiet, and empathy, while showing awareness and regard for all fellow citizens.

- **Attire**

  According to Driglam Namzha, men are required to wear a Gho, which is a knee-length robe with a belt. Meanwhile, women traditionally wear a Kira, a lower-leg-length dress, along with Honju pullovers. They may also wear a Tego, which is a short silk coat.

Kabney and Rachu

While visiting a Dzong (post), sanctuary, or office, Bhutanese individuals ought to keep up with their clothing standard of the Gho and Kira. Ordinary citizens should wear a kabney, a white crude silk band with borders from past on the shoulder to inverse hip, with different shadings saved for authorities and priests. Ladies must wear a Rachu; a tightly woven material hung over the left shoulder at whatever point they decide to go to a Dzong or a sanctuary while showing up before an undeniable level of authority.

- **Eating conduct**

  Eating conduct incorporates keeping up with etiquette while having dinner, be it with high authorities or with family. Prior to eating, one needs to go to God. While eating, the sound, as well as an exaggerated act of chewing, is considered problematic. We ought to continuously take the perfect proportion of food to fulfill our cravings, consequently not squandering any. Likewise, we should not be making looks of fortunate or unfortunate preferences while eating. Under Driglam Namzha, we ought not to begin eating before higher authorities. The oldest in the family eats first. Furthermore, one ought not to sit with the legs crossed in case one is sitting on a seat or a higher seat.

- **Approach to strolling**

  Strolling without cognizant, running while at the same time strolling, making a noisy clamor with our strides, taking huge strides, holding your hand on your hips and running with others, holding hands with companions and strolling, and keeping your hand at your back while strolling are completely considered as uncouth. One should stroll without making clamors, and keeping in mind that strolling with high authorities; one should stroll on the left behind them.

- **Approach To Sitting**

  While sitting before bosses, one ought to keep up with our stance. One ought not to fold our legs or incline toward the divider. This sort of conduct is considered discourteous. Assuming one is perched on the ground, one ought to sit with crossed legs, floor with the hands collapsed, and resting in front. Stooping physically low is likewise viewed as terrible conduct.

- **Approach To Looking**

  One takes a gander at individuals with various types of articulations. For instance, looking with care, sympathy, and love or looking with a furious face. Whenever one is meeting individuals interestingly, one ought not to take a gander at them with outrage. All things being equal, one should check them out with adoration and care. One ought not to look straight into the eyes of the great authorities, and one should be bringing down our look towards their feet.

- **Approach To Bowing**

  When in front of the king and bowing down to him, one should cover our mouth. One bows to the king and high authorities for the purpose of regard for them. One should have the bowers twist their back and head lower while bowing to the king. One ought not to bow to higher authorities before the king. The manner in which one bows to the king and high authorities is unique. When without a Kabney or Rachu, one should cover their mouth and bow.

Verbosity – How One Talks

As indicated by Driglam Namzha, one ought to keep up with dignity while talking and talk as per reality with a cognizant psyche and reflection. One is also expected to talk plainly to get what one means.

The manner in which one talks with seniors: one should converse concerning lamas, high authorities, guardians, and elderly folks.

The manner in which one talks with individuals of a similar age: one wants to converse with our companions or individuals as old as us with adoration and warmth.

The manner in which one talks with the more youthful ones: one wants to converse with more youthful ones with empathy, value them and guide them by offering great guidance.

Lying, brutal words, spreading tales, embarrassing, conniving, allegation and maligning, and mumbling are viewed as terrible approaches to talking and must be kept away from consistently. One really wants to invite a visitor, regardless of whether it is a high authority or an average person, with a grin and approach them with deference.

Psychological – Having A Decent Outlook

The physical way one conveys themselves and a decent approach to talking aren't sufficient. As per Driglam Namzha, one wants to have a decent outlook, a psyche that ponders the government assistance of every conscious being. The inward psyche, Driglam, implies the manner in which Bhutanese individuals think: their affection for the nation, king, and individuals and their regard for the nation's guidelines and principles.

Regard for the national dress is central since it is an interesting personality of the nation, and the equivalent ought to be applied to the national language Dzongkha. There must likewise be the readiness to serve Tsa-Wa-Sum (king, nation, and individuals) however much one can and to have the determination to fulfill everybody. Having a decent outlook assists with keeping up with great associations with everybody and being faithful to companions, life partners, guardians, and oneself.

Driglam Namzha is an affable method of individual turn of events.

With more openness to the rest of the world, Bhutanese individuals invest heavily in Driglam Namzha as a remarkable personality of Bhutan and advance it as an upright set of principles, yet additionally as a marker of Bhutanese character. Driglam Namzha was talked about commonly in the parliament, and goals were passed on its protection and advancement, essentially to check the attack of Western culture.

More or less, Driglam Namzha manages to eschew unrefined and awful physical, verbal, and mental practices and take on common and gracious behaviors of the body, discourse, and brain.

The seniors and the heads of the nation should follow the code of etiquette since they set the model for other individuals to follow. It is an affable method of individual turn of events and a socialized instrument for the agreeable working of the general public. Its inherent worth lies in its being a declaration of politeness, affability, appropriateness, decency, and class. By seeing this esteem, Driglam Namzha can be supported and celebrated as a special Bhutanese legacy.

These policies on the forefront sound like a great idea. However, the intention behind these policies was to strictly target the Lhotshampas and the culture that they brought with them when their forefathers moved to Bhutan because of the previous kings who welcomed them generations ago. It was targeting them and trying to eliminate any other subculture that evolved out of Bhutan. Subcultures sometimes mean the dissolving of one big culture, and if that culture were to be dissolved, then the very fundamental Bhutanese hierarchy would be shaken like never before. It was an attack, perhaps a preventive attack to make sure that things were not acceptable to a certain hierarchal lead.

These policies went as far as regulating infrastructure and architecture as well. It has been reported that this code of conduct, along with all its cultural rules and regulation, worked towards constituting and creating a setup regarding religious, military, and social affairs, amongst many other things. These were all put together under one umbrella of understanding known as "Dzongs." This has been the case since the year of 1998.

Not much has changed for the Bhutan of today as the state continues to promote the ideology behind Driglam Namzha. It has been made an absolute marker of their identity. It is taken up in the parliament at regular intervals, but substantial legislative change is yet awaited.

Chapter 6

New Citizenship Act

Before implementing the 1985 and 1977 Nationality Acts, the Bhutanese Citizenship Act was passed in 1958 by Druk Gylapo Jigme Dorji Wangchuk. As per the act, Lhotshampas were considered the state's citizens if they were settled there before December 31, 1958. The enactment of the laws gave more freedom to Lhotshampas to come into politics. After all, during that time National Assembly was inactive.

Furthermore, the five-year plan was made in 1961, and the road was built completely, which linked Thimphu with India. These reforms gave Lhotshampas a gate to get involved in major activities of Bhutan and settled in North from South Bhutan. Initially, everything went unnoticed, but soon, it came into the observation of Drukpa and especially the government when they started playing an essential role in politics.

That was when the new Citizenship Act 1977 was introduced that restricted Bhutanese citizenship conditions. In the new act, government employees could be given citizenship if they were in service for fifteen years, and if the civilian applied for citizenship, they had to be a resident of Bhutan for at least twenty years.

In the 1977 Act, people were required to write and speak Dzongkha. And that's where many Lhotshampas had difficulty. Yet, they received citizenship as they could prove their residency and land tax receipts before 1958. Because of being Nepali speakers and belonging to Nepali culture, they had minimum or no knowledge of Dzongkha, although many had lived in the state for generations.

The act was the first step to creating the troubles of Lhotshampas that aggravated when the census was conducted, and identification cards started to be distributed. My parents received a Bhutanese citizenship card in 1982. However, at that time, the census was not completed, and ID was not distributed to everyone. The new Citizen Act 1985 was enacted, that restricted the citizenship conditions more.

Initially, in the 1958 Act, a Bhutanese man's children would be Bhutanese if he married a foreigner, but the new law changed the conditions to the opposite. It was when many elites and middle-class Bhutanese used to marry Indians or Nepalis. Thus, because of the new law, they won't become Bhutanese, and their wife had to go through different processes to become a citizen. Besides, people had to be proficient in Dzongkha, and if they had spoken or written anything against the king, then citizenship could be revoked. The government even passed the marriage act that snatched all right from Lhotshampas and threatened their freedom from the core. It made them second-class citizens in their own state.

The new definition did not consider South Bhutanese or Lhotshampas as citizens of the state. Therefore, the government wanted to find out who the people were. That's how the plan was crafted to conduct a census in 1988. The government selected some people from each district and created a census team from them.

The family member had to come in front of them and prove their citizenship. They were required to know the national language and settled there for more than fifteen to twenty years. In the case of Lhotshampas, they had to show their tax receipt from 1958. Therefore, it created problems for them. They thought that it might be the movement of the government to reduce their population, but the government considered it a must to reduce illegal immigration. However, the majority of Lhotshampas have been there since the seventeenth century.

The census was another step to denationalizing Lhotshampas (citizens of Bhutan) in their state, which was apparent when the definition of citizenship was changed and classified into seven categories.

F1- Genuine Bhutanese

F2- Returned migrants

F3- people not available during the census

F4- a non-national woman married to a Bhutanese man

F5- a non-national man married to a Bhutanese woman

F6- children legally adopted

F7- non-nationals (migrants and illegal settlers)

The categorization allowed the government to evict them and snatch their rights. Thus, they provided them with the easiest route to call them non-citizens. In many families, each member fell into a different category which created more problems as families got separated.

Census became the source of information for the government based on which identification card was provided to the citizens.

In my family's case, we were dropped into the F1 category because my parents had identification cards, and we had tax receipts from 1958. However, my grandmother was considered illegal because she was not able to produce her birth certificate, which eventually failed her to generate a certificate of origin from the police station.

The situations and decisions of the government have to be judged from different perspectives because they are related to the national security and prosperity of the citizens. However, if Nationality law would be judged from any perspective, they might be prosperous for North

Bhutanese who were considered true citizens, but they were problematic for Lhotshampas.

The alterations in the law from 1977 to 1985 were the first step to their eviction, which later got strengthened when the census was conducted to denationalize them. The identification cards were not issued to them. Therefore, they had to run to get a Certificate of Origin which created other troubles. To get a CO, people had to go to their birthplace and then come back and ask the police officer to generate the certificate.

An identification card is physical proof of your being a citizen of any country based on which people get a job and other facilities. Because of being declared non-nationals, Lhotshampas had no identification card. Many of them lost their jobs and eventually became unemployable.

Its absence snatched their right to education because schools also demanded parents show their ID cards.

Therefore, many of them left the country in the 1990s, but some stayed there. Now, many of them want to go to a foreign country, but they do not have a passport as their citizenship was confiscated. After all, they were not able to generate CO, due to which they did not get ID cards. That's why they had no way to go out.

Although the laws assisted other communities to excel, the cost was borne by Lhotshampas, who was not at the mistake that much as they were shown. It would be true that the true culture of Bhutan was under threat, but it could be protected through different schemes rather than targeting Lhotshampas.

Their categories corroded the whole generation of Lhotshampas who were and are still suffering, but no one is there to support them, and Bhutan is not even giving them a single concern still.

The census and growing violence against Lhotshampas affected the community psychologically and socially, losing their basic rights. Eventually, the situation worsened, and that increased aggression among people. Out of so many Lhotshampas, Tek Nath Rizal, Royal Advisory Council member and a few other people stood up for their people's rights and talked to the king about people's insecurities regarding the census.

The government might not be in the mood to listen to anyone and found rebelling against him. That's why he was arrested. Some months later, he was released, after which he went to Nepal. And that became the starting point of his activism, yet it was slowed gradually when Nepali police seized him and sent him back to Bhutan. There, he was imprisoned till December 1999.

Yet, his beginning and voice aroused many other activists to come on the street and speak for their rights. However, those activists made so many Lhotshampas come out of which many were uneducated and unaware of what was going on.

The protest raised different demands ranging from basic rights to cultural freedom. They wanted the government to let them wear their clothes and speak their languages. The activists presented their demands to the district headquarters across Southern Bhutan.

The policies of the Bhutanese government might strengthen Drukpa culture—the culture of northern Bhutanese, but the plan threatened the security of Lhotshampas, which made activists come out. Yet, they could come out alone because Lhotshampas were not ruling elites, unlike Drukpa.

That's why they brought educated and uninformed Lhotshampas out of their home to protest with them. Although it created a long march and movement, it did not give the result they wanted because the government was threatened by it.

The Home Minister received a letter from a district head in which he suggested hiring people to find out who was involved in the protest. The government had to take steps; eventually, they hired people from different districts and tasked them to find core members of the movement.

That was the focal point when police and investigators started targeting people and participants of the protest. They were harassed and beaten by the police. Many of them were arrested and imprisoned. There were thousands of Lhotshampas whose houses were targeted, and people were made to leave their houses.

After getting so much violence, many left for Nepal to seek asylum. In many cases, the family leader left the country, after which other members were forced to go to Nepal or India.

The army was at the forefront of targeting their houses and imprisoning them. They forced them to leave, and that's how they started fleeing. Some remained in the state, but their situation was before us. That's how they achieve their motive, reducing their population.

In conclusion, it can be said that Bhutan is different from other countries that have the same population. Because of having a plural society, the government needs to use the principles and techniques of consociationalism in order to have a just and democratic government.

Bhutan is the canopy of Drukpa and Lhotshampas; both had distinct cultures and customs and lived in the state for decades. Lhotshampas culture is more related to Nepal, and Drukpas have Tibetan culture. The government started to feel threatened when Lhotshampas came to the forefront. Thus, they did not know how to bring Drukpas to the forefront, and that's why Lhotshampas suffered.

However, it was wrong to use any of the policies to force them to leave the country. And that's what the government did. The His majesty allowed Lhotshampas to have citizenship and live there. He visited Southern Bhutan himself and met Lhotshampas, asking them not to leave the state because they were its citizens. The Lhotshampas' geo-location facilitated them to hone their skills and played a significant role in the nation's progress. However, the government failed to help Drukpa to work proactively for the betterment of the nation.

That's why the government became threatened by Drukpas, who thought that the Lhotshampas would overtake them. It could be revealed from the letter sent by Deputy Home Minister Dago Tshering in 1990 to Dzongdag in which it was specifically written that a large number of Southern Bhutanese would be considered Bhutanese.

Therefore, the Nationality project was enacted, under which they changed the definition of Bhutanese citizenship and divided Lhotshampa families into seven categories. Their project involved marginalizing Lhotshampas and then forcing them to leave the state.

This might be based on their intentions to protect the country from the social triumph of Nepal over Bhutan, but their result was different.

In my opinion, their policies and amendments were pretty harsh because, in their own country, Lhotshampas were living as second-class citizens with no basic rights or freedom.

The policies could be enacted differently to give freedom and ground to Drukpa to participate in politics. Besides, both communities could provide a platform to represent their culture. Media platforms could be utilized to portray and promote Drukpa culture. The state could use tools and techniques to have friendships with Lhotshampas to build trust, as it was the easiest way to keep the nation safe without harming any other community.

Lhotshampas contributed a lot to the government because of their intellect and proactive role in the nation's politics, but Bhutan destroyed its stance on Lhotshampas by implementing harsh policies. Some writers and analysts presented biased opinions by victimizing one side completely.

In some cases, the government's actions were justified because they had to keep their nation safe. However, there is a need to execute the research process before launching assaults on Lhotshampas due to their immense contribution to Bhutan.

Chapter 7

Ethnic Cleansing

Tek Nath Rizal

Tek Nath Rizal was a farmer in a village who was selected to represent Lamidara Sub-Division in the National Assembly. Yet, his work impressed the king, and with so much effort, he got elected to the Royal Advisory Council in 1984 to represent Chirang and Samchi.

Rizal was quite vocal about different issues regarding identity cards and border demarcation. Besides, he wanted the government to work on increasing the embassies of other countries in Bhutan.

Therefore, the king had high hopes for him and gave him the task of heading the audit teams of developmental projects that began after 1981. This task made him find flaws in the system, due to which he found out how many executives were misusing the funds, including Prince Namgyal Wangchuk, Rinchen Dorji, K.D. Tshering, Zimpen Dorji Gyaltshen, and many others.

The audit was quite long, and when it neared its end, the government decided to have a census in 1988 based on the 1985 Act. With the motive and goal to depopulate Lhotshampas, the community was targeted and harassed as the government adopted new policies regarding the census. Ultimately, Rizal tried to tell the king about it. After all, it created chaos in the public, who already disapproved of them on social grounds. After listening to his opinions and ideas, Rizal was ordered to submit everything in the report, so he did as directed. He submitted the petitions, which were forwarded to the cabinet. Later, Gup Wangchen informed him that the king did not want him in the Cabinet meeting.

The submission of the petition and the intense investigation that went into it left him with many enemies. Consequently, he was banished from his position, and afterward, he was arrested. In prison, he was tortured and grilled for information he did not have. He was released after three days conditionally after signing a confession agreement.

Protest and Demonstrations

Lhotshampas went through a lot, due to which they started protesting and had demonstrations to get their rights. The protest was not that well organized, it was not well planned, and the leaders of the protest were told that they were going to come and address the rallies in various parts of Southern Districts, but no one went to address that rally because it wasn't organized perfectly.

In 1988, they submitted a petition with the help of Tek Nath Rizal and B.P Bhandari to the king in which they explained what they faced because of the census. Instead of listening to their grievances, the councilors were arrested.

Hence, the community protested primarily in 1990 on September 24 and October 4 throughout Southern Bhutan against the implemented policies; their protest was peaceful until the army attacked the demonstrated. In one of the protests, Lhotshampas burned the traditional dress when the government made it compulsory to wear it. Thus, the September and October mass demonstration organized in 1990 created more spark.

During the mass demonstration, the leaders circulated the controversial pamphlet, *"The Gorkha People of Southern Bhutan Must Unite and Fight,"* which side-eyed the Drukpa culture. Because of its content, it was not focused on giving Lhotshampas their fundamental rights, but it was more about their dominance.

The establishment was afraid of Lhotshampas' domination, and these protests made them believe that their fear was justified. Subsequently, they made every effort to force them to leave the country. The army forced them to sign emigration forms to move them out in many cases.

Demonstrators and Army

Demonstrators had the agenda to get basic rights; therefore, they protested peacefully, but the army created chaos and started beating them.

It did not start so suddenly, but the by-product of the coordination between the Home Minister and Village leader. One of the village leaders sent a letter to the home minister in which he told him about the demonstrators and asked to arrest them.

Subsequently, the Deputy Home Minister sent a letter to the District Head and asked him to take action against the demonstrators. That's how the protestors were attacked by the army and police, and mass arrests began with inhuman torture without due process. Schools in the southern districts were converted into temporary Army barracks. Parents were concerned about their children's education and safety for their life.

Police and the Army

The demonstrations did not result in what they really wanted. Instead, the government got stricter. After those protests, the government thought Rizal was behind it; therefore, he suffered more behind bars.

Meanwhile, it was made compulsory for the public to get a No Objection Certificate (NOC); otherwise, they could not get an education, scholarship, medical insurance, job, visa, or any government service.

Those people who were still in Bhutan and their family members became refugees; they did not get NOC just because their family members were in refugee camps. Without a NOC, they neither get a passport to travel nor do they have legal grounds to stay there.

Moreover, police forced the demonstrators to leave; they were tortured and harmed to make their families leave their homes. The government, in response, took their properties and made it useless for them to come back to get money.

As per the campaign, they were forced to leave the state; the remaining or residing Lhotshampas were marginalized in hopes of bringing Drukpa to the forefront.

In conclusion, we can say that the fear of the government was justified, but their approach was brutal. Their strategies could be soft or more accommodative, or conciliatory to mutually promote acceptance and tolerance rather than suppressive and outright authoritative.

However, their fear didn't help them in the long run. Their gentle approach could help them get the favor of developed nations and better relationships with other countries.

Chapter 8

Meetings

Considering Lhotshampas as the threat was the issue the government had deliberately created in which none of the developed countries were willing to take part. The Lhotshampas people had become refugees, but India was not ready to host them because of its friendship with the Bhutanese government. Playing its diplomatic cards, India avoided all kinds of involvement with the issue, not willing to risk its friendship with Bhutan.

Meanwhile, Nepal made every effort to make refugees' lives easier. The two had around seventeen bilateral meetings regarding refugees or Lhotshampas. However, neither India nor international organizations like UNHCR, the EU, the USA, etc., participated in them. That was the primary reason why the bilateral meetings failed to make better decisions.

From 1990 to 1993, the king visited southern Bhutan many times and asked southern Bhutanese not to leave the country and refer to them as Bhutanese citizens. After sixteen rounds of bilateral negotiations between the government of Nepal and Bhutan, nothing substantial was achieved. Bhutanese refugee leaders requested the government of Nepal to include them or the international community at the negotiating table. Nothing such ever happened that is of my knowledge.

However, the authorities did not give importance to them, due to which no refugee leader was allowed to participate in the negotiation conversation. Consequently, it angered the leaders as they thought they could explain the situation better than government bodies because of their first-hand witness to the chaos.

It all happened because Bhutan was directly or indirectly involved in practices to take out Nepali- speaking Bhutanese citizens from their country. The leaders who participated in the eviction of Bhutanese refugees were leaders in the Joint Verification Team representing Bhutan, presuming that they had a responsibility to address the issue of Lhotshampas. Because of their biases, Bhutanese refugees knew what they would face later because of the verification team. Unfortunately, they were right in many ways because the verification team put a large number of refugees in the category of voluntarily migrated category even though they were verified.

Bhutanese leaders failed to provide Lhotshampas with basic rights; therefore, the Nepali government took steps in favor of Lhotshampas, but their efforts turned futile. Currently, the issue is still unsolved.

Ministerial Joint Committee

The government of Bhutan and Nepal formed a joint committee, Ministerial Joint Committee (MJC), in 1993 with the motive of solving refugee issues. After conducting meetings with the committee, they decided to categorize the refugees into four types and then see who could be brought back to Bhutan.

1.   Bonafide Bhutanese (evicted forcefully)
2.   Bhutanese who emigrated themselves
3.   Non-Bhutanese people

4. Bhutanese who were involved in criminal activities

Nepali leaders, or the government of Nepal, agreed to the categorization without consulting with Bhutanese refugee leaders. They were heavily criticized by the refugees in their own country because they all knew that the Royal Government of Bhutan would classify most of them into other classes, not consider them Bonafide Bhutanese.

And it happened; after the visit of American representatives, the two countries conducted a joint verification in a camp where refugees were living. There, they categorized them into four categories; for example, in the Khudunabari camp, there were around 3158 families and 12,183 individuals, out of which only 293 people or 74 families were considered Bonafide Bhutanese.

After so much effort from the Nepali government, Bhutanese leaders were ready to bring them into their country. Still, they did not have the freedom as they had to wear the traditional dress, speak their national language and obey the rules they had made for Lhotshampas. According to the press release of the MJC, emigrants could reapply for their passports and residence, and criminals could try to prove their innocence, but non-Bhutanese had to return to their countries.

Therefore, class 2 became a significant concern for international communities because the military and army tricked many Lhotshampas into signing papers that said they were leaving the country happily. Therefore, they could not prove why they wanted to come again. Moreover, they were required to return to Bhutan to apply for citizenship.

Verification system – flaws or the best?
The verification system was filled with flaws; it categorized most of the refugees as emigrants or criminals, even though many had lived in the country for decades and centuries.

However, on the other hand, it worked as proof to show the king that the refugees were, in fact, Bhutanese, not outsiders. If they were not Bhutanese, why were they living a refugee life and dying to go back to Bhutan? Moreover, contrary to Bhutan's claim, the majority of them were found Bhutanese citizens even though they were put into category two.

The other proof is from the king, who went to Southern Bhutan and requested people to stay there because they are Bhutanese. And the letter of the Deputy Home Minister, Dago Tshering stating "a large number of Bhutanese people have left the country, and they will no longer be considered as Bhutanese citizens."

Hence Bhutan lied a lot in terms of Lhotshampas; they kept saying that they were not Bhutanese, but the reality was the opposite. It was proof of their devilish plots to throw Lhotshampas away.

Census and Lhotshampas

Census was the reason why there was so much chaos. There was tension before it even commenced, and when its report was out, there was anxiety all around as many Lhotshampas were not considered citizens. As mentioned in previous chapters, they were sorted into seven categories, and many of them were made to leave the state. They were tortured and harassed.

The reason to consider them criminals and immigrants was to get an easy way to force them to leave the country by making their lives difficult. They were then not allowed to come back to the country, and if they dared to do so, they were arrested and given life sentences. More than 50 political prisoners are living inhumane lives in various Bhutanese prisons.

Conclusion

In conclusion, it can be said that despite having so many bilateral meetings and organizations to resolve the issue, Lhotshampas are still suffering. There was no unity among the organization, which made their opinions feeble and fraught with discord. Even now, international organizations, as well as India, largely refrain from getting involved in the issue, knowing full well that their involvement might help Lhotshampas' case.

Chapter 9

My Life in Bhutan

Bhutan has become a land of tyranny, but being my home country, my emotions are still connected to it. Any news about it rolls me back into memory lane, giving me a ride to my childhood memories and the friends I made there. There are some painful memories due to which we left the village, but between those troubling days, we had some loving memories with friends and parents.

My grandparents were born in the 1930s in Bhutan, while my father in 1957 and my mom in 1962. They had also lived in Bhutan since their childhoods. My parents did not have a life of royalty. My dad wanted to study further, but he could not because he had siblings, and my grandparents wanted his support to manage the expenses. Thus, Dad got his first job. He did not study after fifth grade and stayed home to support his family.

Our home was in Samrang. It is where I opened my eyes when I was born; we had a pretty happy childhood. I still remember how I used to go to his workplace when I was six or seven years old. He was a clerk there, working as hard as possible to fulfill our needs.

Our house number was 202; the government gave us that place. Before I was born, the government opened a new settlement on the eastern side and offered us a home there. And my family availed it at the very moment. After all, owning a property is important to get citizenship.

Our neighborhood was different from others if I compare it with today. There was a forest near our place that had a lot of elephants; that's why Dad roofed the roof with tin, and the walls were rock walls. We had rock walls to provide protection from elephants and ensure that they wouldn't break them. Besides a strong tin roof, my parents used other ways as well. We had many acres of land, and Mom would plant a small area of rice for elephants, assuming that elephants would eat their own portion and not destroy the others.

My dad had a hectic job. He returned home on weekends; hence, we were forced to use different ways to keep us safe from elephants. Even though we used multiple solutions, Mom, my siblings, and I had not had a sound sleep because of their noise and the fear of elephants coming into our home. I often get confused whenever I find things different from others in my childhood, but time is the best way to understand some things.

I had two brothers and a sister; one of my brothers died at the age of five. My siblings were no less than a support system for me. From joyous moments to hard times, we faced everything together; that's what made my childhood memorable. Childhood is always special because you have no idea about anything, so you enjoy everything without any perspective. Probably that's why I enjoyed going to school and staying at home, working with my mom on chores and cooking. I enjoyed being her helping hand. In school, my friends gave me so many things; although we used to go there for a few hours, we played soccer and rock stones together. Frisbee was also our favorite sport, yet soccer was our life.

Racism and discrimination were not even our thoughts. Our class had Drukpa kids, and we did play with them and made them part of our games. Even though they spoke different languages, we did not give that any value; we just valued our enjoyment and memories. Maybe, that's why innocence is a blessing. Unlike government and politics, we were there whenever anyone needed help or support.

There were lunch breaks and breakfast times in schools in which we used to get food from our school; it was the most enjoyable moment for us. At times, we were sent to fetch firewood from faraway places so that staff could cook food for us. It was another roller coaster ride for me because we used to talk and share jokes on the way. Cleaning was another activity in our school, and we all were keen or rather forced to participate in such activities. Thus, our usual chores were to clean the classrooms and toilet. And if we got failed any test, then we had to clean others' classrooms.

Life was somewhat heaven for me; we had farmland where there were pigeons and cows and everything. Being connected to nature is also a blessing, and I had that blessing. There was a personal and social connection; everything was there. Yet, things changed after March 3, 1990.

Chapter 10

Immigration

Bhutan was special for me, but sometimes you have to leave your special place for a better future. Some memories and places hold a special place in our hearts, not because they are good places or joyful memories but because we have spent such a long time in those places that the heart has grown fond of them. Bhutan was the same for me; I spent the most precious time there, but the country did not remain like its beautiful self after the mass destruction. Even though we were the legal owners of our land and property, we were still forced to leave the country.

My dad was a clerk in the office at the Samrang Coal Mine, which is at Samrang (Bazzar) market. It was attacked, but Dad somehow managed to come out of it safely.

The next day, there were troubles all around; I was in school with my friends when we heard the sirens of army cars approaching the area. My friends and I were children, so they left us, but they took some teachers hostage in their cars.

I had no idea what was happening or why they were doing it, but I was afraid for myself and my siblings; therefore, we all ran home. Even though we safely reached home, I was still afraid about what would happen next. Dad, at his place, had so many things to deal with. The following day, he went to the office; it had been destroyed, and all the offices near them were also ravaged.

He started working in the destroyed office when some high-positioned government people came to the place. They investigated the place and thought that Dad was behind the destruction. Dad could not prove his innocence; therefore, he was beaten and kicked so brutally that he was severely injured when he came home. The government people had given him two choices, either stay in Bhutan and face the punishment, or leave the country.

Living in the state was not a good option; it would be riskier. He picked the second option and became a refugee.

We all have a history of migration. My great-grandfather's parents lived in Nepal, but they came to Bhutan when my great-grandfather was four years old. He grew up and lived there till his death. My grandfather and grandmother were born in Bhutan in 1930, my parents were also born there, and as you all know, I was born and raised there as well.

Due to the situation, we decided to leave Bhutan for good. Although there were no large protests in those days, opposing parties were demonstrating in small groups; the situation was not only alarming, but it was terrifying. When Dad came home injured in the middle of the night, he said nothing but announced that we were leaving. My siblings and I had no idea where we were going, but we could see our parents rushing to pack things and leaving food for our animals and birds in the courtyard to eat. Within minutes, we left for an unnamed place by my dad's friend's truck with merely a few bags. We snuck into India by foot and set out to Nepal.

The journey was bitter and harsh as we had no food or water. Mom did not come with us. Dad had planned to return to the country after three days as he thought things would get a little settled after three days. It was not wise to think like this because political matters cannot be settled within three days. Most Bhutanese were unaware of the political crisis at that time, or they could not realize that such scenarios take time to settle; my dad was also one of them.

We traveled to India and later to Nepal overnight with hunger and thirst, thinking we could return to our home after three days. However, it took three months to bring Mom to us. There was nothing but a barren land when we arrived in Nepal; no camp, no food, or water. The truck dropped us at the border town of Nepal. We had brought nothing with us, so we were forced to ask people around us like beggars for food, but there was no help. Fortunately, crossing a little distance brought us near a Hindu Temple. There, we got food, water, and sound sleep at night while being unaware of our true destination.

We needed to find our true destination where we could live, build our shelter and grow crops. Staying in the temple helped us in some ways. It brought us near a person who suggested my father go to Barney. We were helpless and had no choice but to do what others said. So, we did as that guy said. We went there, and it helped us. We found a village head who gave us his land on rent, where we started doing fieldwork. The menial work helped us make a living, not a decent one, but we were thankful for what we were given. Initially, we did not have anything, but now we had something. If we compare our lives in Nepal to Bhutan's, we had to start everything from scratch.

Immigration is always painful because you have to start everything from scratch, as we and many people like us. It was not so long before we noticed other Bhutanese coming to Nepal. It had become more like a community of Bhutanese there. Dad used to help them by bringing them together and helping them live with us. Soon, they started flocking and doing fieldwork with us. Later, a refugee camp was made near the riverbank, Timai.

The camp formation was truly helpful; international organizations like UNHCR started coming to help us. Besides, the location helped us grow crops and flock together. Initially, there were ten families, but soon, it grew to thousands of families. Education and management issues were also catered to after the camp formation.

It all happened in 1992; before that, everything was terrible. Our houses were made of bamboo poles after the camp formation. Before 1992, we used banana leaves and branches to create shelter for us. Some teachers were also living as refugees there. In the beginning, they used to teach us under the big shady tree.

There were no washrooms near our classrooms, but there were forests. During break time, we used to go there to play and pee. Therefore, the place had no hygiene, which became the main cause of death of many children there. Kids used to get dysentery and diarrhea that took their lives. Yet, school time was good. We used to get Unileto from foreign organizations; it used to be a mixture of flour, water, and corn flour.

Everything started to get better, but our lives seemed stationary as we did not have our mom with us. After three months, Dad went to Bhutan and brought Mom before the refugee camp was started on the Timai riverbank. We were excited that Mom would be here with us, but the reality depressed us. A few days after our departure, the government destroyed our house; Mom had nowhere to go. She used to hide in forests during the daytime, and she used to sleep in our neighbor's home at night.

When Dad went to our village, he found her in our neighbor's place. He did not wait for a second and brought her to Nepal to live with us. Her presence brought euphoria to our lives; after all, moms are home, not a shelter.

We spent the worse days of our lives in Nepal near the Timai River in our refugee camp. In those days, I used to crush rocks near my camp and sell them to help my family. I had some friends there who used to live like me in the refugee camp. We used to play soccer, but dirty drinking water took their lives; some died of cholera and some diarrhea. In those days, there was no clean water to drink. I remember the days I played soccer with other friends and saw foxes and jackals unearthing my dead friends' bodies and bones. It was a horrible experience for me. It seemed I was the luckiest; that's why I was saved.

I studied there till grade ten with the desire to move to another country where we would have better facilities for higher education, yet Dad was not ready for it. Nepali or Bhutanese culture was different from other countries. Parents were more protective of their children even when they became adults. Therefore, they want their children to take permission from them for everything. The first time, in 2002, I applied to go to Canada, but my application was declined, stating that I would be repatriated to Bhutan as negotiations were going on between Nepal and Bhutan. Later, I tried to resettle in the US early in 2007, but my dad did not give me permission; my siblings also wanted to go to the US, but Dad managed to make them stay there. I was a fearless son who used to think that I would be able to adjust to a foreign country if I could adjust and live in a refugee camp with no identity for twenty years from 1990 to 2009.

Dad unallowed me, but I still sent my application on my own, and IOM accepted my application. I was twenty-five years old, which meant I was an adult and could make decisions independently. The approval allowed me to move to the US after many rigorous interviews with US government officers. The flight took me to Atlanta, Georgia. It was not like New York or California or the mind-image that people had painted of the US. Instead, I got an apartment in a big building from where I could see big trees and animals. As soon as I got there, I called Dad to tell him about my journey. I told him what I could see from there, and he was confused, "Are you literally in the USA?"

He thought the US would be like a city of lights with many industries. He was right, but not the whole US is like this. I ensured I was in the US. Life in the US was also not a bed of roses; I worked hard to build my life here. I had multiple jobs along with full-time classes.

During that time, I made an effort to make my family come there. Although they came there, it was another struggle for them because migration demands you to start your life from scratch every time. And we did this with the hope of having a better life than before.

Chapter 11

Life in the USA

Living for nineteen to twenty years in a refugee camp and then coming to a place where you don't have to make an extra effort to fetch water is something. It was difficult to adjust to a new place and adopt the new trends and situations. I was in the phase of a quantum lift. That's what I called it because I came directly from refugee camps to modern America.

Our life in Bhutan was limited to our farm and house. We did not have to look for a job to make money because we had our farm where we used to grow crops to feed ourselves. We had our own home and property, so we never had to worry about rent. But all the chaos in Bhutan forced us to become refugees in a matter of days.

We were solely dependent on foreigners to provide us with our basic needs in a refugee camp. We were provided with basic food after every fourteen days, but the food supply was very limited, and we had to be cautious about the way we used it. Therefore, we needed a source of income. After passing tenth grade from my refugee camp, I started teaching at the remotest place in Nepal. Since I was a refugee, I did not reveal my identity. Because of the lack of systematization, I did not have to verify my identity, which helped me teach students. During my time as a teacher, I taught at different places. Whenever I used to resign from the school, I informed them about my identity.

At that point in time, we still did not require a job because UNHCR was there to fulfill our basic necessities. There were people who really needed a job, but there were no jobs in the camps; why would there be? Like every refugee camp in Bhutan, most of the refugees were wasting their human resources, skills, and labor, even though they could be utilized creatively to help them meet their expenses.

Due to the unavailability of jobs and policies restricting them from working, many people used to go to different parts of Nepal with fake identities to be able to work. I also hid my identity and worked in Nepal for five years as a schoolteacher.

We lived there for many years; we worked there and completed our education. I did my bachelor's (undergraduate degree) outside of the camp, and my siblings completed their high school and early education. Since growing up, I saw educated people wearing clean and tidy clothes; I thought of being a doctor when I grew up, and that's why I continued to pursue higher education. I always wanted to remove the refugee tag from my name, which is why I wanted to go abroad.

My siblings were also like me, but my dad refused it. However, I was different and had already made up my mind to move to another country. Dad was afraid to go out. After living for many years in the refugee camp, UNHCR offers the families three options; go back to their home country (repatriation), get affiliated with the host country (assimilation), or re-settle in a western country (resettlement). My family was given an offer in 2008, but everyone denied it. However, I was stimulated to go out.

Many Bhutanese refugees, including my family, wanted to return to our country, but it was not possible to use that option. That's why we chose the last option. The option of repatriation had not started yet, and no country was helping the remaining refugees with that option. Thus, many are still living in the refugee camps with no help; all to go for repatriation themselves.

Since 2003, I have been looking for ways to move out. Initially, I applied for a Canadian visa, hoping to have a better life. But my application was rejected; the authorities stated that Bhutan and Nepal were having meetings to resolve the issue.

Later, I entered into the refugee resettlement program in 2008 because I was an adult and had the right to do it. It is easy to wish to migrate to a better place, but it is way too difficult to go through that process. I realized this when I had to go through the said process after my application was accepted.

I just filed a declaration form stating my wish for resettlement. IOM did everything, from paperwork and traveling cost to choosing a country for me. Therefore, till the last moment, I did not know that I would be transferred to the US until IOM gave me a paper stating that they were sending me to the US. The news was a synonym for the euphoria to me. My happiness knew no bounds; I could not sleep for three days, telling my family and friends that my days of suffering were gone now.

The background check process was quite lengthy as the authorities wanted to know the logical reason for my leaving Bhutan. I explained to them that my family and I were pushed out, due to which we had no option except to look for shelter for us. I told them that my dad's office was destroyed overnight, and government officials threatened my dad's life. This made them believe in me, and they let me go.

The process did not end there; the interview had questions about my work experience and education. At that moment, I thought they would just be typical questions, but they were building my resume and sent me to the state that had opportunities related to my field and career. Therefore, I was placed in Atlanta, Georgia.

I was teaching and studying in Kathmandu during my whole resettlement process. For the final US Homeland Security interview, I was in Kathmandu. I left for the interview by bus without knowing that there was a strike in Tarai by Maoists. At that time, Nepal was in the middle of the Maoist revolution. As soon as our driver knew there was a strike in the next town, he arranged a fake bride and bridegroom to show that the bus was not regular. The strikers eventually let our bus enter the neighborhood. Yet, later, they discovered it was a fake during the inquiry. Soon, they asked us to get off the bus and set it on fire. The next day, I had a final interview that could change my life. There were no means of transportation then; therefore, I started walking along with other passengers.

I walked that whole day and night in the woods. It was scary, and I was afraid for my life while remembering my early refugee life and the death of my friends who I used to play with. The next day, I arrived at the UNHCR office and told them about the chaos I faced. Eventually, the receptionist agreed to postpone my interview.

After my interview, I thought that I would not be able to see my motherland; therefore, I planned to see Bhutan. I visited in January to do a final see-off. I entered Phuntsholing and watched a Bollywood movie, *Baaz*, at Norgay Cinema Hall. There, I made a few Bhutanese Nepali friends while watching the movie. I told them that I was from Samrang but currently living in India. After the movie, I walked over the bridge to the hill near a school in front of wood factories. It was a sad day, and I was still looking for ways to return and help my fellow Bhutanese in any way I can.

As I stood at the gate, my heart weighed heavy with uncertainty and a deep sense of nostalgia. The crisp afternoon air seemed to carry a bittersweet fragrance, a blend of the familiar and the unknown. This was the moment I had both dreaded and anticipated, leaving my homeland for good, not knowing if I would ever return. With a heavy heart, I took one last glance at the country that had been my home for a few years but had a deep respect and eternal longing. The flag waved gently in the breeze, and I whispered a silent farewell, not knowing if I would ever see it again. As I stepped into Jaigon, I carried a mixture of hope, trepidation, and a profound sense of gratitude for the memories and experiences I was leaving behind, ready to embark on a new chapter in my life with the world as my canvas.

While exiting from the Indo-Bhutan Phuntsholing gate, border security bid me goodbye. I looked back at them, smiled, and responded. With his accent, I could tell he was not Nepalese. I did want to talk to him, but I was afraid to do so as I was there without proper documents.

On February 24, 2009, I stepped into America, dreaming that it would have nightlife and skyscrapers, but all turned in vain when I journeyed to my home and found wild animals and a forest near my residence. The residing place differed significantly from my home in Bhutan and the refugee camps. It was big and had electricity, running water, and everything that was unavailable in Bhutan and makeshift camps' houses in Nepal. My case manager taught me how to use the toilet, stove, and rooms in the US.

My father could not believe I was in the USA; he thought the authorities had transferred me to another corner of Nepal. He had a fear that authorities won't fulfill their promise as he had listened to multiple stories and experiences like this. However, I made him believe that I was in the USA.

Coming into the States was not the final goal or end of life; it was the beginning of another life. Life was about nothing but making money and fulfilling necessities. Thus, a job is essential as money defines your choices. After resettlement, I started looking for jobs. My first job was at a clothing store where I arranged clothes according to their size.

The job was not of interest; I knew I deserved something better. After all, I had a bachelor's degree, and my master's degree was near completion, with majors in Political Science and English. Yet, you can't get anything so easily and quickly. I ended up with a job at a clothing store as I was not in the position to wait for something related to my prospect.

I was hopeless when I joined the store, but I gave it my best. Yet, I could not please my manager. After three to four weeks, the manager came to me and said that I was not fulfilling the task efficiently, so he decided to shift me to another department. I was given the task of cleaning the washrooms. It was worse; I did it for three days, after which the manager fired me. That day, I cried hard; I was torn when I looked at the mop in my hand. I did not tell my parents about my job.

I left for home with the hope that things would go in my favor. Some days were spent at home, sitting idle. But after four or five days, I got another job in a grocery store where I had to stack things. The owner used to pay me $7.25 per hour. The work was easy, but the pay was insufficient to meet my family's needs and support in Nepal. Over the night, I used to listen to rap music and learned some moves, even though I barely understood the song. Later, I started to pick up its lyrics. I mostly enjoyed 50 Cent, Eminem, and Hip Hop, R&B. It helped me learn English.

So, I started working as a server at a small fast-food restaurant in the daytime. I also made $7 per hour over there. Still, the money was insufficient as I had to pay rent, bills, and other living expenses besides helping my parents back in refugee camps.

Lack of money always creates stress and tension, and so does more money. I was broke; in such dire conditions, you tend to seek help in your surroundings. I did not know any Bhutanese in the USA as I was new there, but I was connected to some through the phone in New Hampshire. One of them was a friend in a refugee camp. Our fathers knew each other, and both of our siblings studied together. We were great friends; the best part was that she understood me.

She suggested I move to New Hampshire as it had better job opportunities, and the pay rate was reasonable: $10 to $11 per hour. Your best friendships have the quality to convince you, and she convinced me to think about it. But more than this, she convinced me to think about her too. A companion is needed all the time, and I needed her. One day, on-call, I proposed to her, and she said "yes," but she also asked me to talk to her dad.

We grew up in a Bhutanese household with a Nepali culture where parents have the right to marry a child. They are the ones who take full responsibility for finding the best wife for their sons and husbands for their daughters. She did what society had taught us, and I did what she had asked me to do. I talked to her dad; her dad subsequently asked me to speak to my dad. After talking to both of them and fulfilling their demands, the two happily agreed to our marriage.

During that time, I decided to move to a new place, and on December 5, 2009, I achieved that goal and stepped into New Hampshire. New Hampshire was lucky for me as I married my friend on December 12, 2009.

Changing the city is not enough to give a turn to your life; you need to make other changes as well. My goal was to earn money but also do something I had an interest in. That's why I enrolled in a training program related to licensed nursing assistants. After becoming certified, I started working at two places to make ends meet. One of my jobs was at the hospital, while my other job was to help high school students find jobs and homes of their interest. The second job was quite interesting. I had to give them orientation and take them to different places. The work was simple, and the pay was good.

There was an incident I faced there that I could not forget. I took nearly twenty-five high school dropout students to clean Hampton Beach. One of the girls refused to clean the beach, so I asked her politely to show up, but she was not ready. Subsequently, I asked her for an explanation. While answering me, she used so many filthy words that I had never heard of. Eventually, I deescalated the situation by calling the office and asked the supervisor to pick her up.

Life was quite busy; I had two full-time jobs and a college education. I started going to Manchester community college. Later, I transferred to Southern New Hampshire University to finish my undergrad degree. Hence, my wife and I did not get time for each other as we both had jobs and were busy. But it yielded fruits as I completed my degree after a few years, and it helped us start our own business and resign from our jobs. Everything took time.

We both tried to bring my family to the USA during that time.

Initially, my family was not ready; they thought there would not be a Hindu temple, so they could not pray. It took time for my wife and me to help them understand, but two years of effort was worth it because, in 2011, they came to the USA and started living with us.

Coming to the USA was a dream, but every dream has a cost. Before arriving there, the authorities gave us an introductory orientation session in which they showed us the positive side of the USA, making us think that the USA was no less than heaven. Still, when I came there, the land was opposite to what we were told. It was also home to problems, from poverty to racism to the healthcare system; everything was flawed. It would help if you constantly tried to make your lives stable there.

Besides, you have to learn the culture of your new country and get used to their slag and etiquette. I was pretty naïve when I came to the USA. I was unaware of their slags and how they talk, thinking that I know everything about their country. But I was wrong, and I realized that when I got in trouble.

At times, people crossing the roads used to say hello to me and ask, "Whatsup?" I did not know its meaning, so I looked up at the sky, thinking they would have to show me something above the ground. I would end up relying on them, "There is nothing in the sky." Because of the communication gap, they all said only hello to me.

At the grocery store where I worked, I often made several customers return because of *Yogurt*. Later one of the customers complained to my manager regarding this. The manager took me to the Yogurt aisle and asked me, what is this? Without hesitating, I answered, *curd*. Eventually, he got furious but taught me that curd is called yogurt in America.

Hence, a huge communication barrier between me and the commoners affected my ability to adjust there. I could not understand their words but did not realize it until I had to visit the doctor once for an appointment.

The receptionist let me go to the doctor, but she asked me to bring an interpreter. I kept resisting, but in the end, she asked me if I could understand what she was saying. That made me realize the need to learn English.

However, I learned things with time after realizing what I did not.

The best part of the USA is that you can live life with dignity and respect as you can earn money and work there, but in Bhutan and Nepal, people are limited to living as refugees or second-class citizens. The USA gave me a new way to live, but it was just a door; I crafted my way myself.

Chapter 12

School

The memories of school, made with friends and classmates, have always remained with me. Those were the moments when we were ourselves and cherishing the present moment. Adulthood is when you must be conscious and thoughtfully make the decisions that guarantee a better life or some future fruit. But school life is when you learn to live in this world; thus, you have more ground to make and learn from mistakes. And this ground of mistakes gives you the freedom to enjoy and cherish more.

Rushing to the USA after twenty years of life as a refugee gave me a chance to study in college in the USA. And it was a completely different experience for me as there was a vast difference between the schools of Nepal and the West. It took me a great time to settle there. After all, I was from a refugee camp, lacking all resources available to everyone, even in third-world countries.

Exams were the biggest difference in Nepal and American schools. In Nepal, we used to have one annual exam; if you failed, you would stay in the same class. The same practice was followed in college too.

Yet, in America, there used to be exams every week or month, which helped students score marks throughout the year based on which they were promoted.

The biggest problem I faced was language barriers; I was in a community college in New Hampshire and had a public speaking course there. My teacher was friendly, but there were some communication issues between us. To make the class engaging and students to participate, he gave us examples from cartoons and series that were watched by average Americans.

I was raised in a refugee camp, so we had no newspaper, radio, TV, or internet to surf the news so I could not imagine watching their cartoons. Hence, I could not relate to the examples he used to give to teach us tricks and techniques to talk to people effectively and convince them.

Public speaking classes were not solely theoretical; we had to talk in front of the class and discuss some of our memorable incidents. At times, it seemed I was the only person who could not enjoy the class. It became a great hurdle with time. However, those hurdles made me sound different as I had other stories about those regions they were unaware of.

Most of the students were Americans; their experiences were also related to where they grew up; fortunately, many could relate to it. But, I used to share my experience of Bhutan and Nepal with them. It was very different from theirs, so they used to give me their ears. Sometimes, it seemed I was a gateway to impart some additional knowledge to them. But, in most cases, I could not find myself adjusting to them.

In one of my class speeches, I told them that I lived in a refugee camp for almost two decades near the riverbank, where I used to catch fish, fiddlehead, and wild mushrooms. In that speech, I told them how Timai River was a natural swimming pool for me. When I told them I did not have to pay rent there or spend money on food, they looked at me with awe. Everyone got eager to go there. But later, at the end of my speech, I revealed that I was in the refugee camp. It was nice to see their face when hit by my unfortunate reality.

I used to tell them about monarchies, the religions we used to practice there, and our lives in the refugee camp. I told them about our habit of catching fish for food and how it was not fun. It was a different experience for them as they had never had people in their neighborhoods living in the camps without facilities. Thus, my stories sometimes attracted them, which was a plus point.

American schools were too different from Bhutanese schools. Although I studied in a refugee camp, teachers used to explain and describe every line of our lessons. They used to give their perspective, and we had to accept those explanations. We used to pay all our attention in class, but in the USA, students seemed not attentive in class. They used to share their critical opinions with the help of examples and the theories they had read.

It was somehow shocking because we did not have resources. Still, we showed interest, and they had resources but ignored their studies. The reason could also be a job, but if they wanted to pursue their education, they would be attentive in class. Many used to be busy texting others or in pastime activities during class.

The other difference was the dress code; in Nepal and Bhutan, we had uniforms or a specific dress code to follow in school: white shirts and black pants. In the USA, it was the opposite; students could come in flip-flops and half-pants. Initially, it puzzled me, asking me why they were coming in such clothes. But with time, I realized that their system is different from mine. It is freedom.

Thus, the education system is organized differently than in the USA. Students did not know, at times, what had to be taught, or they did not get homework. In a refugee camp, we could only study until grade ten. Afterwards, we had to go outside the refugee camp to study in college to complete grades eleven and twelve. Later, we could go to a three-year college to complete our bachelor's, then complete or enroll ourselves in a master's degree program.

I studied until grade ten in a refugee camp. It was a good time; we used to get there on time, updating our teacher on what was taught and what had to be taught in the class. The teachers would give us homework and ensure that we were progressing. Physical punishments were given if we failed to be present in class on time, get done with homework, or provide satisfactory answers to the teachers. We used to be punished for skipping class, cleaning the toilet for a week or more, kneeling outside the classroom, or help teachers do their personal work.

One of the teachers forced us to fetch bamboo from far away forest to build his house. We helped him construct his house. In return, he used to give us notebooks, foolscap papers, and good marks in our exams. Most importantly, he would not beat us if we failed to do our home assignments or answer his questions correctly.

America had well-built and managed classrooms, but they lacked patterns. That was the problem I faced there to adjust to my college.

It was challenging in the USA for me to achieve grades. As I said before, I was naïve and unaware of their system. I did not know if I had to write long answers or if teachers would give me decent marks on short answers. Besides, I was unsure if I could write or provide examples of my experience in Nepal to make my answers worth reading. I did not know much about issues in the USA, so I could not write or give examples, and that's where I got stuck.

However, time is the best solution for many things. I learned at my pace to achieve grades; I had to read many books to get accentuated with American issues and cultures. Fortunately, my efforts brought fruit, and finally, I graduated from Southern New Hampshire University and Norwich University with a good GPA. It truly felt like a great success.

Life was pretty harsh in Nepal. We did not have enough money to hire a tutor or get more resources to study better. There was no electricity in the camp, so we had to rush for Kerosene oil and study under the dim and flickering light of the oil. And when the oil got exhausted, I had to sleep without completing my lesson.

Dad used to work in a refugee camp to make some money, but we struggled in many aspects. So, schooling was not exciting or filled with carefree moments. It was another name for tensions and worries.

And almost every family had its struggle in the refugee camp. Study probably felt important but something like a burden. Hence, completing it would not feel like success but a moment where you can relieve yourself that you do not have to run for kerosene oil anymore. Therefore, it was not celebrated. But in the USA, the graduation ceremony was celebrated grandly.

My parents and family were here in the USA during my graduation ceremony. It was great and overwhelming to have them with me at that moment. I was the first person in my family to complete an undergraduate degree in the USA. It was the happiest day of my life. But nothing ended here; I did my master's, and all went well. Thanks to my writing skills, I was not bad at writing English, as English was the medium of instruction in schools in refugee camps. Practice made me perfect, but speaking was the hurdle. My naivety was the proof of it. Thus, everything was done in academic life with pretty grades; whatever I got or experienced, I enjoyed it. After all, they were teachable moments for me!

Chapter 13

Marriage

Marriage is an institution that guarantees peace and harmony, yet you have to cultivate it and work on it as a builder to get the desired results, or else you will get tangled in problems.

My wife was an important part of my life, especially when I came to the USA. I don't think I would've excelled much if she hadn't been there to listen to and guide me. The moments when we were together metaphysically were the moments when I realized I had to marry her. And it was the best decision I ever made.

Our love story is not so different from others; it's a cliché. The word cliché sounds boring or something stupid, but deep inside, we love clichés that make us feel warm and fuzzy.

Our dads have known each other since their school days. That's why our families are no less than family friends. My wife and I were born in the same place, Samrang. Both our families moved to Nepal in the early 1990s. It seemed destiny had already decided to bring us together.

In Nepal, we all lived in the same refugee camp, Timai. Her brothers and I were classmates there. She was not a part of my childhood memories because of the age gap; I was nine when she was three. She was a child with whom we played during our free time.

Time passed, and her brothers and I moved from the refugee camp for higher studies. It was a challenging phase of my life as I could not contact my family. We had to change and lie about our identities, or they won't let us work and study there. I was doing my bachelor's there while teaching during my free hours. Therefore, I portrayed myself as an Indian guy. So, there was zero contact between me and her during those few years. But it did not feel much because she was not an essential part of my life then.

Later, in 2008, I returned and found something shocking and okay to digest; her family had moved to New Hampshire. However, it did not affect me much as we had no connection. In 2009, I also moved to Atlanta, Georgia.

I think it was the point when destiny played its game. Life got pretty difficult for me in Atlanta as I did not know anyone and could not earn much. So, I contacted her after some time to get some help. That's how I got connected to her and her brothers.

It was a time when I used to talk to her on the phone. I used to share all my problems and chores with her. And it was very heart-warming. She became my friend, and eventually, I found my love for her. One day, I jokingly proposed to her, "Would you like to marry me?"

I thought she would reject me, but she did not say anything. Instead, she asked me to talk to her dad. Right away, I understood her intentions. In our culture, parents decide for their children, and children do not dare to cross the boundary. It is a sign of respect for their parents.

After some days, I did what she said. Her dad did not say yes or no but asked me to talk to my dad. That night, I called him in Nepal and spoke to him about the proposal.

Soon, both fathers talked it out, and my dad called me and said they all agreed to our marriage. That call was memorable for me. I soon moved to New Hampshire, as it is somewhat like Bhutan. My wife helped me find an apartment there and prepared everything for me before I moved there. In the same month, December 10, 2009, we got married. My in-laws were very supportive; I was pretty close to them.

My parents moved to the USA in 2011; they lived with us. Having them with me was very helpful as my wife and I had hectic lives. After marriage, I was enrolled in a training program and had two full-time jobs. My wife also had jobs so that we couldn't manage the home and children. My parents were like my children's caregivers, whose presence greatly relieved us.

Later, they moved to another state in 2012, and things got a bit difficult as one of us had to stay home and look after the children. However, things eventually started getting better. We started our separate businesses, so we did not need to go to the office for work. She started her beauty Salon while I started a Human Service Agency.

We now have two children, and both of us have successful businesses. My ultimate goal is to complete my doctoral degree and work in the peacebuilding or conflict resolution sector.

Chapter 14

College

We give importance to those things that have value in our parents' opinions. My dad always regretted not getting a chance to complete his formal education even though Bhutan had a modern education system in 1961. Because of being the breadwinner, he had to discontinue school to feed his siblings and send them to school.

Although his siblings are very educated today, one is a physician, and others are highly educated, the credit goes to him for their success. He felt a bit of a failure for not achieving what they achieved. My uncles and aunts may have a different perspective on this.

Similarly, my mom could not study from scratch; being a daughter in the 1960s, she was supposed to serve the family and dedicate her life to the kitchen and home, so she was not sent to school ultimately.

Their regrets and unfulfillment created the value of education in their opinions that ultimately transferred to us naturally, and sometimes, parents transfer such things to us through their habits.

I was in grade nine or ten and loved to play soccer, volleyball, and table tennis. Mom and Dad always used to push me to study. I was not a bad student in school but had to repeat grade eight when I failed exams. That gave my dad a reason to push me harder.

One evening, I came home after playing volleyball, and my dad was angry. I sat down to read and do my homework. He began giving me a lecture, stressing the importance of education. I mimicked him, thinking that he was not looking at me. He saw it and started spanking me with his slippers. He was so angry that he did not let me in my room all night. We had a small corn field at the back; I uprooted all the corn plants and stayed in the toilet until midnight. Later, I snuck into my room.

So, that was the major incident that instilled the value of education in my heart and soul.

My parents used to make every effort to help us continue our education. They came to the USA in 2011, and their support mattered a lot to me because, without their assistance, I could not have completed my bachelor's degree. After all, they were to babysit my kids when my wife and I used to be away for work and studies.

Many could not manage to study with their family and job responsibilities, but my support system was so firm that I completed my goal with two jobs and my family. All the credit goes to my family.

I completed my bachelor's degree in Nepal but moved to the USA without completing my master's. Life in the USA was pretty tough for some time, still had a goal deep inside to complete my education. Later, I moved to New Hampshire. Life started getting easier. I made some quite helpful friends. One of them used to study at Manchester Community College. One day, I went with him to the college and showed him the administration records of my bachelor's and incomplete master's degrees.

There are some differences between Nepal and the American education system, because of this I had to start my university education from scratch. Nepal's bachelor's education is three years, while in America, the same degree is four years. The administrator asked me to enroll in a bachelor's program. It was not happy news for me, but I pacified myself that it would give me a way to learn more about the Western education system.

The initial experience of studying in the new system was challenging because of language barriers, and I did not know their college systems. Unlike others, I did not have a high school in the USA. Usually, high school students tour the college to get guidance on what they would learn or experience at the new educational institute. But I jumped into the new pace with zero direction. That created some trouble. But things started becoming easier after six or seven months.

During those months, I finished some of my credit hours in the community college. After some time, I realized the need to transfer to a better university; that's how I landed at Southern New Hampshire University. There, I completed my remaining credits. I even had online classes there.

Online classes were pretty cool; even though we could not see each other and had some differences of opinions, at some points, we used to discuss something different that could bring us all to one page. I used to discuss South Asian politics and cultures as I had no idea of USA politics.

I completed my undergraduate degree in two years; I learned a lot of things from the incidents and events I could share with my classmates and the knowledge I gained from them. Besides, my inflexible schedule taught me a lot of things.

After graduation, I aimed to do a master's in International Relations or Foreign Policy, but only a few universities offer such programs. One of them was Norwich University, a military and civilian university. I was in its latter section. It was a different experience having drills and seeing many students wearing military uniforms.

Norwich University taught me many things. In other words, it enhanced my knowledge about global sectors, how states function, push and pull power influence, and many other concepts that helped me expand my perspective on international politics and anthropological behavior.

That master's was beneficial for me as I always wanted to participate actively in community work; my degree helped me work in the presidential campaign 2020 as deputy policy director at Bernie Sanders's movement in my state. My goal was to involve myself in national politics and work in the human rights sector at an international organization, peacebuilding, and conflict transformation sectors.

My academic progress made my parents the proudest; it was evident during my graduation ceremony when they were happy and celebrating the day. Thus, it was not my victory only but a victory for my whole family. Without them, nothing was possible.

Chapter 15

Career and Business

Life is always uncertain, but we never think about that when making plans for our future. In Nepal, I imagined teaching English in college and university after my master's. That's why I majored in English and Political Science in my undergraduate degree. But things and plans changed when I moved to the USA.

The struggle of resettling here made me directionless for some time because my motive was to earn enough money to pay rent and support my family for a few years. That made me hunt for jobs and agree to work anywhere willing to pay me. But if I see it in the long term, my move to the USA developed my interest in politics and encouraged me to know more about the problems the nations are facing and how they can be solved through peacebuilding.

Yet nothing happened in a day; I first went through a struggle to find a job to help myself and my family; that's why I went through a lot by working in a clothing store that made me feel inferior, especially when my manager asked me to clean restrooms even though I had an undergraduate degree. Later, I had two jobs to have enough income to pay bills, but nothing worked. I felt like a failure at that moment because I got nothing even after moving to the world's richest country. I was still struggling, failing to pay bills and support my family. However, my struggling time won't remain for a long time. After all, you learn to cope with them and find a way to fix them.

My life started changing when I enrolled myself in college. Later, I moved to New Hampshire, and there, I realized that learning short courses could help me double my income. During my job hunt, I learned about a nursing course and how much it could increase my pay. Eventually, I enrolled myself in a one-month licensed nursing assistant course. After a month, fortunately, of the course, I got the job, and the pay was too good.

However, my wife and I never stopped attending college and achieving academic goals. We worked at different places for a long time, exploring ourselves, but later started our businesses. My wife had a license as esthetician; after working in salons for years, I encouraged her to be her own boss. And she did that in 2018. Still, she has been actively working on it, and I am motivating her to open its other branch in a different state.

The year 2018 seemed to be our year; we both began our journey as businesspersons. My interest developed in Human Services after doing a licensed nursing course. I thought of starting a business when I was in college. I even started the process of market research and found the importance and benefits of the human service business.

My motive for starting a business was not to earn profit, but to serve society, the society that accepted me or welcomed me as their own when I had nothing. In 2018, after graduation, I started a Human Service Business with my friends, having two to three people in our office. Our work comprised of helping the elder community in their daily tasks. Today, I am still working on that business; it has grown much today with dozens of employees in our office.

Working in this industry helped me understand the core problems of society, and that's what gave me a way to involve in politics. During the presidential elections, I became part of Bernie Sanders' campaign.

During that time, my friends managed the business operations. Thus, working for yourself never goes waste; it always leads to the places and things you are interested in. An example of my business is in front of you which helped me get involved in US politics. New Hampshire helped me meet several political figures like Hilary Clinton and brought me to a place where I could work with some known figures regarding the problems Bhutanese face. Yet, for this, credit should be given to my friends or my business partners, who were there to manage all operations when I was busy with presidential campaigns. I am now associated with many international organizations to fulfill my goals, solve global problems, and make our only planet a better place to live.

Chapter 16

Work With Senate And Realization

Government can bring change if it properly utilizes all its powers. I always wanted to shed light on and make the people of America aware of Bhutanese refugees and their problems. Being a refugee, it overwhelms me that no developed nation supports us or steps forward to bring peace and harmony between the Bhutan government and Lhotshampas, people of Nepali origin so that they can have a peaceful life.

I have always been interested in international relations and politics, thanks to being a Bhutanese! Fortunately, I cultivated that interest and tried to achieve my dream. My dream was simple; educate people about Bhutanese issues.

Nothing happens effortlessly or rapidly; everything requires hard work and time. My participation in community activities helped me excel in this field. It helped me make contacts and create my networking circle; this circle helped me achieve my dream. I participated in several election campaigns, and beyond that, I knew some politicians in New Hampshire.

In late 2014, I called Senator Dan Feltes; I knew him personally and asked for an appointment. The next day, we met in Starbucks as per his request. There I told him about my aim to educate people about Bhutanese problems and humanitarian crises so they could be rescued. Fortunately, he liked my idea and asked me to prepare a draft. I did not know the basics of draft preparation, so I asked him to guide me.

With his help, we talked about ethnic cleansing, political prisoners, refugees, and human rights problems Bhutanese had faced in Bhutan. A resolution was created; and all senators and representatives voted for it in the house.

After the resolution is produced in the NH state, I brought a group of Bhutanese high school students to one place. I drafted a sample email and asked everyone to send it to 400 NH House of Representatives and 24 Senators. It was the first Bhutanese's engagement in the legislative process. Students got new experiences and learned how to engage in politics. Eventually, our resolution was put into the consent docket, which means there was no disagreement.

The resolution resulted from the sponsorship of major Democrat and minor Republican leaders. Soon, the resolution was passed in New Hampshire after so much effort. We got positive notes and reviews from numerous Senators.

And with that dream in my heart, I moved forward. I got to work with US Senator Jeanne Shaheen, who later sent a letter to the Prime Minister of Bhutan on our behalf. Yet, the Prime Minister of Bhutan's response was not positive enough to welcome. I heard from my sources that Prime Minister, Tshering Tobgay, commissioned his people to find out about me. Finally, he falsely claimed we left Bhutan in 1991; I was not a Bhutanese citizen. He also did not find the correct names of my parents. Both of my parents' citizenship cards attached here are proof of my nationality.

Later, the NH General Court sent our resolution to President Obama and the response of the Prime Minister to the US Department of the State. We did not get feedback or further steps to address the situation, but the engagement was done frequently. I tried to contact them and call the White House, but due to having no contacts there, I could not get a way to connect to them. However, Secretary Kerry's office later sent me a letter citing the lack of a US embassy in Thimphu, so we could only do limited things.

I did not know about the peace and reconciliation approach and its benefits then. It's a famous saying that always start early; the project or your dream will automatically help you find a way. My dream and intention were to educate the masses. And with that dream in my heart, I moved forward.

We even sent a letter to the then Prime Minister of Bhutan. The letter was effective as we got a reply a few days later. In that letter, he considered my family and me illegal immigrants. His response agitated me. I took my parents' citizenship cards provided by the Bhutan government to the state departments and told them that we were born in Bhutan and we were Bhutanese citizens.

I wanted the state department to take action because my mom and dad wouldn't be allowed to meet their relatives living in Bhutan if my family and I were considered illegal immigrants. During those years, I even went to Nepal and met with the former Prime Minister of Nepal and asked their help with peacebuilding. PM KP Sharma Oli blatantly rejected support for the peacebuilding and reconciliation concept. He stated how you can leave everything and reconcile with those who exiled you. I insisted to him that the government of Nepal and the Maoists fought decades of revolutionary war, thousands died. Eventually, reconciliation was been achieved, not entirely, though. However, the option you have chosen was the reconciliation.

In those years, I met several politicians. We discussed Bhutanese refugees' problems and the need for developed countries to help them fight against the humanitarian crisis. In 2017, I got to participate in a congressional hearing. It was three days in which we discussed Bhutanese problems from different perspectives. We discussed the mental health problems we had been facing due to statelessness and separation from our loved ones.

From the Peace Initiative in Bhutan, eighteen of us made a trip to Washington D.C in 2022. We imparted a lot of knowledge and understood others' perspectives on the issues. We met several political figures like Senator Sanders, Senator Schumer's staff, the Speaker's staff, and others. We asked for help to build positive peace and reconciliation by instituting the Truth and Reconciliation Commission and adopting a congressional resolution on Bhutan. Currently, this resolution is in the US Congress. It is at the Senate Foreign Relations Committee and House Foreign Affairs Committee. During that phase, we built a lot of connections. Through this advocacy to resolve the Bhutanese issue peacefully based on mutual trust and understanding, we reached out to many high-level influential global leaders and organizations, including the European Union *South and South Asia*, the United Nations, and other peacebuilding transnational organizations.

I even got to talk to the Prime Minister of Bhutan, Lotay Tshering. The day he won his election, we talked about Bhutanese issues, during which I also wished him luck for his tenure. I also spoke about the ongoing pain and suffering of the Bhutanese people. Whether outside or inside, thousands of families are divided, which affects their emotional well-being.

That day, I requested him to allow resettled Bhutanese to visit Bhutan and allow reunification. The other two issues I raised with him were releasing the political prisoner and resolving refugee problems. I also stressed on the "Happiness" of the people of Bhutan. His answer was substantial enough to believe.

In the end, he thanked me. He said, "Thank you for your call, Suraj. I heard you. We do have this problem. I will do whatever I can to resolve this matter."

He gave me his email address, but I could not connect with him as he did not reply to my emails after that conversation. I did not think it was professional to call him again and again. But we sent him a "Peace Proposal" along with the King of Bhutan on behalf of the Peace Initiative Bhutan. All went unanswered.

Learning and engaging with peacebuilders helped me understand the importance of a peace and reconciliation approach. It made me realize that our government never gave importance to peacebuilding with Bhutan, due to which there were problems. Once, I went to Nepal and cited their example of reconciling with Maoist. Although the meeting did not go well, it built my interest in peacebuilding.

Our concept was to build peace between the government of Bhutan and the Bhutanese in the diaspora based on mutual trust and understanding, finding common ground, and healing the people and the nation. For outsiders, the country is happy and free loving. Undoubtedly, we, Bhutanese, love nature and peace, but there is chaos inside our place.

Chapter 17

The USA And Developed Nations

Behind the growth of every developing country, many developed nations play a role. At times, they helped through money and sometimes through their skills. Besides, international organizations are always there to lift them. However, the case of Bhutan was too different. As it is an isolated country, most countries do not know about the situation of their refugees.

Moreover, during the late 1900s, the world was already in trouble due to Gulf War, the genocide in Rwanda, and American Operations in Africa. So, it is obvious why the international community or foreign countries would notice Bhutanese refugee problems, which are not as large in number as other countries suffering at that time.

Thus, the first was to make them aware of the Bhutanese situation. And once it was done, no organization who were asked for help ever declined the needs of Bhutanese. Numerous countries came to help Bhutanese refugees; the example of America, the United Nations, and EU is in front of us. However, the problem was that the countries assisting the Bhutanese refugees continued to fund Bhutan, due to which Bhutan did not make an effort to facilitate refugees.

Later, communities were formed in developed countries to help Bhutanese in different ways and create good ties with remote places. During the expulsion, the Tom Lantos Human Rights Commission sent a letter to the King of Bhutan, but it did not result in the expected results. Bhutan simply ignored it.

Bhutan's neighbors have played a significant role after people learned about the issue. India was one of them. However, India has motives to help the nation and fulfill its needs. Bhutan's budget relies mostly on India. You can say that India is their mother, and India loves to support them so that the neighboring country won't go to China for help. After all, India and China are competitors.

America, similarly, has been playing an important role in distributing food to Bhutanese. Besides, one of those countries offered us a resettlement program. However, it was not appreciated much because people, especially the older generation, thought they were detaching them from their hometown. As discussed in previous chapters, the example of my own family could help you understand it pretty well. None were ready to move to another place except me, as I wanted to free myself from the refugee tag. The USA gave me the opportunity to do that.

No doubt, in the beginning, the journey was challenging because the state was not like heaven as told by people during the orientation. But I got a job there, which helped me gain independence and support my family.

In contrast, the program was effective and beneficial, yet people giving orientation should give fair information to help people make a decision. They just tell Bhutanese positive things about America, due to which people develop high expectations. Ultimately, they would receive a cultural shock when they come to the place. The same happened to me when I came here. I thought that I would get a better job, but none of my educational records were valued as I was given the job of cleaner and stacker initially, which was something that I did not like.

Yet, things improve when you work hard and dedicate your energy to your goals and dreams. Those dreams were why I established myself there and convinced my parents to come. They eventually came there after two years and their presence helped me to excel in my career and academics.

The USA welcomed me openheartedly; it provided a way to earn money and establish myself. That's why within a decade, a majority of Bhutanese are now successful today and are resettled in America. Many are entrepreneurs, and some have excelled in academics. Thus, the resettlement program has proven very helpful for the Bhutanese. It helped people like me to rebegin our lives. Hence, our only option was to go to other respectable nations where we could improve ourselves. The USA gave us that direction.

Chapter 18

Peacebuilding

Conflicts are omnipresent; they exist everywhere in this world. But that does not mean that they must remain. There are ways to resolve them; one is peacebuilding and reconciliation.

As a person who grew up around chaos, it was not so easy to realize its importance until I took part in political activities and observed how politicians made campaigns and made an effort to achieve the desired results. It helped me realize the fact that we could resolve the problems of Bhutan through peaceful techniques, as the politicians' gained votes without bullets through effective campaigns. It made me look for alternatives, and that's when I learned about peacebuilding and reconciliation.

We all know that the government of Bhutan and Lhotshampas have differences; many were exiled from their hometowns and abused. It is scary, but the two parties must come to one table and talk to resolve the matter. But none is ready to talk and solve the problem.

Communication is the way to resolve the issue, and that's what peacebuilding is all about. It is about sharing your opinion and giving ground to another party to express their thoughts. Hence, it all could be done through dialogue.

Therefore, my team and I started networking with other people in Bhutan; our first steps were limited to talking to our friends and family members who were living in Bhutan. Later, we started sending proposals to approach other people. The first dialogue sessions were not about resolving conflicts but more related to the impactful role Bhutan has played globally. Such sessions helped improve mutual trust and brought the two to one table. After all, their support will create an environment where the king and the ministers would feel comfortable discussing the issue and give them ground to give solutions.

Our strategy was simple; it was about setting grounds to bring the government and the nation to the table to talk because we knew that if reconciliation is reached, more than 115,000 resettled Bhutanese whose families are back in Bhutan would be helped, and Bhutan would have a different image in the global stage. Therefore, our motive was to improve the relationship.

I strongly believe that Nonviolence, peacebuilding, and reconciliation represent the best pathway to healing and resolving longstanding conflicts. These approaches are grounded in humanitarian values, emphasizing the sanctity of human life and dignity. By focusing on sustainable solutions, they break the cycle of violence, promote inclusivity and dialogue, rebuild trust, and provide opportunities for individuals and communities to heal emotional wounds. Moreover, nonviolence and peacebuilding align with international norms and laws, receiving support from the global community and minimizing human suffering. These methods not only hold the moral high ground but also offer a realistic and transformative means to end protracted conflicts and create a more peaceful and just world.

Bhutan has become the hub of structural violence today; there are two kinds of violence in general—one is active/hot, and the other is inactive or structural. For instance, the killing of thousands of people every day in Syria or in Gaza Strip or in Israel is an example of active violence, while making new-born child non-citizen because one of their parents is not a Bhutanese citizen is an example of the latter. Similarly, not giving registration to Christian organizations is also structural violence. Besides, the discrimination between Lhotshampas (and other Bhutanese) comes into the category of structural violence.

After all, it is a problem in the structure of society that results in problems and troubles for people who feel abused.

Active violence-related issues can be solved with the techniques of negotiation, and protracted problems like this need peacebuilding and reconciliation because it is communication that helps us to find and address the root cause and form a cohesive society. It will help people build trust. Today many Bhutanese Americans cannot visit Bhutan because the government doesn't issue visas to them. Many people are attached to their hometowns and desire to go there. Yet, the issue could be solved through peacebuilding.

However, it won't happen easily without the support of international peace-building organizations; there are NGOs and departments within UN that are specialized in building peace. Besides, many developed nations have peacebuilding organizations. Their support for the Bhutanese government could bring the government of Bhutan dialogue to solve the issue.

We launched a rally on the International Day of Peace (IDP) in front of the UN Headquarters in New York in 2022 to create awareness among people of the Bhutanese issue and make peace organizations help us bring the government for dialogue. Without the support of large nations, the motive could not be accomplished fast. We are hopeful of achieving our goal and soon will get the support of peace organizations and NGOs.

Chapter 19

Bilateral Talks

Whether it is a petty matter of home between two sisters or parents and children or it is a complicated matter between two companies or countries, communication is the way to bridge the gap and find a solution. After all, conversation brings thoughts and reasons to sealed lips, resulting in understanding the root cause of the problem. It takes time to understand the root cause, but once it's done, the problem presents its solution as well. If not solvable, taking out the issue would be the only task you will be left with.

Therefore, bilateral talks and peace talks are always preferred to bring out the solution to the table. We all are familiar with Geneva Peace Talks on the Syrian Civil War. However, it is found that those talks fail in most cases. The example of the Syrian matter is in front of us where no peace talk could generate a solution.

Despite their inability to generate a solution, we can't say that communication has no power to unite people or turn wars into friendships. The example of Japan and America is in front of us; they were no less than enemies during World War II. Although Hiroshima destroyed the going-to-be booming nation terribly, it was their communication that brought them together and turned them into partners that could not be separated by any power, at least in this decade.

The government of Bhutan and Nepal had 16 rounds of bilateral meetings to solve the issues of exiled Bhutanese, but none was fruitful. The two parties were the extreme opposite; there was and is the need for a third party to help them come to the table and discuss the problem they are facing. The third party could be their neighboring countries like India –one of the largest democratic countries in Asia, due to which they could help a lot or any international organization like the UN or other peacebuilding organizations.

The government of Bhutan never agrees to come to the table to talk; thus, there is an utter need for an organization that could convince political figures to come out to discuss the matter, especially the King of Bhutan. After all, he is the head of the country. Yet, the organization needs to ensure that it won't involve or interfere in its internal politics.

For bilateral talks, we need to build the foundation first where both parties would feel comfortable discussing the matter. Creating or coming to the first step is also challenging as there is no environment for both parties that assist in creating bilateral talks.

According to the intergroup theory or contact hypothesis by Gordon Allport, four conditions are necessary to reduce prejudice or for two conflicting parties to come for dialogue equal status, common goals, cooperation, and institutional support. Bilateral talks mostly fail because of several causes. The peace talks can only be successful if the four conditions mentioned above are fulfilled.

In the case of Bhutan and exiled Bhutanese, Bhutan has, and well-established government, and exiled Bhutanese are no less than 140,000 in total, but they don't have any organization that could represent them. That's why they are not of equal status.

They do not have anything in common, but if you look into the matter from the lens of the psychology of commoners, both parties doubt each other and want peace. And without peace, there won't be a solution to the existing structural violence.

Thirdly, no one has goals to come together for discussion as exiled Bhutanese are not in a mood to solve the problem and the Bhutan government has other agendas.

Fourthly, Bhutan has the support of India in the matters of foreign policy and national security. Yet, the same support system is not there when there needs to be a bilateral talk.

These four conditions form the ground under which the parties can have a conversation or hard talk to solve the matter. Without meeting them, it won't be possible to have a discussion. After all, they serve as the way to build trust between the two problematic parties, and trust is the way to solve the matter.

The most practical tip for organizing effective bilateral talks is when the parties are clear about their stance and have common ground to discuss the matter. And it is possible when there is trust. Trust is not easy to form but when their motive is to build peace, then it can be achieved easily. Instead of benefiting themselves, the aim should be to form peace.

The common goal would bring Bhutan and exiled Bhutanese to the table easily and nearer to solving the existing simple and complex problems.

To address this kind of issue, there are two approaches, top-down approach and the bottom-up approach.

The top-down approach focuses on top main agendas, where leaders from two different parties sit down and negotiate a mutual deal to solve the problem, and finding its components to fulfill the aim. Hence, in the case of Bhutan and Bhutanese refugee, the problem can be ideally solved through it because exiled Bhutanese have citizenship of better countries, so they don't want to come back but want a peaceful relationship with the government and people of Bhutan so that they could visit their loved ones once at least. Yet, this will not address root causes of the conflict, and supplement the process of truth finding, and reconciliation.

Hence, top-down is an easy approach but does not seem appropriate. Currently, the exiled Bhutanese need acknowledgement and apology from the government and the pathway that could help them reconcile with their loved ones.

It has been years since none of them could meet their families, who are separated because of their distanced relationship with the government.

Secondly, the bottom-up approach involves taking the simple and complex steps from scratch to solve the problem. Hence, using this approach is not suitable to solve the issues of exiled Bhutanese because the refugees settled in western countries don't want to come back. Bottom-up approach entails people-to-people relations, bondage, trust among people as integration is their wish or option. And resettled Bhutanese are not looking for integrating with Bhutanese by going there.

They are looking for ways to develop harmony with their, loved ones, and establishing mutual relations would not harm. It is a good thing. To be able to help our families back in the country by building schools, libraries, child play centers, and by helping poor and differently abled people are human values, and we want to do that.

Building peace is generational work; it's time-consuming. The basic reason for building peace is that families separated from each other because of the differences between Bhutan and exiled Bhutanese could meet. The issues need to be addressed humanely based on two motives, families of the exiled Bhutanese and freedom of movement. Otherwise, nothing could be solved even after fifty years. That's why we came up with Peace Initiative Bhutan; we don't want to defeat the government, but our purpose is to improve the relationship between the government and exiled Bhutanese. Its primary goal is to promote positive peace and reconciliation in Bhutan through mutual trust and understanding.

PIB does not have an adversarial approach toward the Government of Bhutan; instead, it seeks to find a mutually beneficial solution through sincere dialogue, compassionate listening, and active participation in a comprehensive peacebuilding process. It plays a positive role in bridging the existing gap between the Government of Bhutan and the Bhutanese in the diaspora. And our belief is that the Truth and Reconciliation Commission will help find mutually agreeable solution, where both conflicting parties win.

After all, the world is nothing without people and what is the use of this technology and advancement when the same people are unhappy and waiting for a long time to meet their relatives and move freely.

Started in 2022, the motive of our efforts is to bring numerous organizations on board to help us solve the Bhutanese problem. Today, there are numerous successful exiled Bhutanese living in America. Through their help, we met Congress and people of the President Biden's administration to discuss the issue.

Communication is key to solving the problems but that key should be used smartly, meeting all conditions or no results would be yielded.

Chapter 20

Diversity with Limits

Countries with one ethnic community are easy to manage and run. But, what about countries having numerous ethnic communities?

You can't manage them and have policies to bring and promote one culture. Instead, the government needs a different strategy to help each community grow and contribute to the nation's economy. Hence, they have to apply the basic and complex principles of inclusion. Such countries have no option except to promote diversity, or the head of the state would be responsible for the cultural genocide happening in Bhutan.

For decades, Bhutan was a canopy of numerous ethnic communities, all living happily and welcoming other communities. Some came from Tibet, Nepal, and others from India. They were like a small community and family, celebrating festivals and living together. They could be used for the country's benefit, but the Bhutanese government's threats and doubts destroyed the diverse nation.

A diversified country can earn a lot because of its culture; people love emotional things, not money, but a country needs money. However, Bhutan lost so many things.

Audre Lorde once said that differences do not divide people, but the inability of people to celebrate and accept differences separates us. That's what happened in the case of Bhutan. The government had an option of accepting the diversity and giving them ground to excel, but their doubts and assumptions saw Lhotshampas more like a threat.

Accepting the differences is not about letting all nations do wrong things, but it is more about giving them space to practice their own culture and speak their own language. There used to be Nepali-medium schools and Hindu temples in Bhutan but all were closed. Recently, a few temples were opened. There is no church because the government tried to unite people under one culture. Their policy's motive was to depopulate people of Nepali origin, who had different cultures, traditions, and languages.

The government of Bhutan once openly said that diversity is a boon in a small country like Bhutan. To the contrary, they implemented policies that aimed to bring all different ethnicities under one Drukpa culture.

That's why today there is chaos. There are nations in the world that have diverse communities. Take the example of the USA; it has communities of Pakistanis, Indians, Arabians, and other countries. Because of their policies—people are excelling and contributing to the economy. Many are in Silicon Valley and generating millions in revenues. Besides, many have their stores and pay taxes. Thus, this has created a win-win situation for the government and the people. Their government promotes diversity and respects all ethnic communities equally. Besides, everyone has equal rights under the law, and they are thriving; therefore, many people want to come to America. Yet, gun violence and racial discrimination make some feel unsafe in the US.

Diverse nations can result in energetic and booming workplaces. The more different the people, the more different mindsets you will get who can contribute the knowledge they gained from their home countries and help the new nation to excel.

Again, take an example of the US here; the Indian residents helped Silicon Valley and tech giants accomplish their goals. The example of Sundar Pichai is in front of us. Inhabiting there since his twenties, he not only helped him to make his career in Google, but it also helped the tech giant to cover miles.

There are also examples of Norway, Australia, and Finland—these countries have diversity that makes a difference and good economies. Australia is the house of different nations, from Chinese to Americans and British. And the best part is that most people feel safe there.

Today Bhutan has only the Drukpa culture; other cultures and ethnicities are subdued and not promoted. Therefore, the current generation of Lhotshampas doesn't know their language, dress, culture, and tradition. They started forgetting their root culture. Hence, it is a mundane nation now with no colors that can attract others to their country.

The Bhutanese government still has a chance to bring their old colors back and promote different cultures to make the country diverse. They can take examples from the countries mentioned above.

Chapter 21

Where Is the Matter Now

Although years have passed, the situation of Lhotshampas is still very depressing. Refugees exiled in the '90s still could not repatriate.

There is a general understanding among Bhutanese refugees that 130,000 were exiled in the early 1990s, out of which 30,000 spread to India.

However, from the refugee community, close to 115,000 are resettled, and 6,500 are still in the camps in Nepal. For years, the refugees preferred the US, but things changed after Trump. Therefore, now in America, many far-right groups think that colored refugees should not come into their country. Or blatantly, they say no more immigrants or refugees.

From 2007 to 2020, we were chosen to leave the refugee camps for the West to live a happy and secure life. I was also one who availed of the opportunity and moved to a better place.

Still, many people live in refugee camps and dream of leaving the country but have no option because the resettling program is over. Currently, 6,500 refugees live in Nepal without any support from international organizations. Therefore, the people are not provided with rations, quality education, and other basic facilities. They are living alone with no job in the refugee camps, which have now become the home of older people, women, and children.

Children and women are vulnerable, having no shelter and basic facilities. Bhutan is the happiest place for others, but if you ask the region's minorities, they will reveal the reality. Unfortunately, none could resettle to another country anymore since 2020. The government of Bhutan fears that the migrated Bhutanese will return to Bhutan. Therefore, they are doing everything to prevent them from coming back to Bhutan. The government uses diplomatic relations with different countries and media policies to spread the lie that Bhutan is the happiest country in the world.

However, resettling to another country is not so easy. People who migrate there suffer psychologically. The biggest reason for some of the Lhotshampas is the language barrier that does not let them communicate with English communicators. Eventually, they could not go and attend parties and meetings. Their anxiety worsened when they could not find a job because of their low educational background. There is a huge difference between Bhutanese and American culture; hence, cultural shock is the cause of sadness in the case of many refugees.

According to research conducted by CDC in 2012, Bhutanese who resettled to the US have the highest suicide rate. Since the late 1980s and early 1990s, over 100,000 Bhutanese citizens, mainly of Hindu Nepali ethnicity, have been forcibly expelled from their homeland and subjected to torture, violence, family separation, enforced disappearance, and even death.

This crisis has had heart-wrenching consequences, tearing apart numerous Bhutanese families and preventing them from coming together to participate in the final rituals of their beloved ones. Almost fifty political prisoners, who courageously stood up for human rights and democracy, have been unjustly sentenced to life imprisonment since the early 1990s. This harsh and disproportionate punishment has silenced their brave voices, advocating for fundamental values. Every day, their hearts ache with the weight of separation, their souls consumed by a profound longing that knows no respite. The laughter and tears they once shared with their loved ones remain locked away in the chambers of their hearts, forever yearning to be released.

The plight of these refugees and resettled Bhutanese resulted in immense suffering and has taken a severe toll on their mental health and well-being. Trauma, post-traumatic stress disorder (PTSD), and family separation have pushed Bhutanese Americans to the highest suicide rate and mental health problems compared to other ethnic populations in the United States. As the Prime Minister of the largest democracy in the world and Bhutan's immediate neighbor, we implore you to intervene and facilitate a peaceful resolution.

Besides, the government has taken their property and changed laws; eventually, they have become stateless.

Unlike Nepal, the Bhutanese government is powerful and well-established in foreign policy and politics; hence, it can influence international organizations' decisions. The international community is not taking bold steps on this problem, as only a few thousand refugees are left behind. Besides, Bhutan has established its name as a happy and peaceful nation.

The other reason behind ignoring the Bhutanese refugees and their supporters is that they are not united; they don't have a representation in the world. Have you ever heard the name of the representative of Bhutanese refugees? No! So how could you expect that people would give value to their issue?

However, the issue is not so simple. There are many other problems. India is also not ready to speak on the matter because of its relationship with Bhutan. Bhutan is its helping hand or supporter whenever it has to face China because of the country's geographical location. India is an influential country; its words will be given attention. Its absence has worsened the situation of refugees from different perspectives.

Solving the Bhutanese issue is challenging because it requires several steps to bring the Bhutanese government to the table to discuss the issue. The motive of both parties should be to find a solution instead of winning over the other.

The Bhutanese leaders and politicians are provided with Western education; they study diversity and inclusion but are not ready to welcome them in their state. Their concept is that diversity in a small country would result in division, the mindset of old English politicians.

Diversity is not about implementing other cultures; it is more about letting people follow different cultures without harming them.

The solution to the Bhutanese problem lies in intergroup contact theory. The theory states four conditions before the conflicting parties meet to solve the problem: equal status, common goals, intergroup co-operation, and institutional support. Meeting loved ones, releasing political prisoners, and finding a permanent solution for the remaining refugees can be accomplished by entering into a holistic peacebuilding and reconciliation process.

Building mutual trust and understanding is a must to come to this stage.

Chapter 22

Bhutanese Community

No one chooses to become a refugee—their circumstances or lives make them.

Many people like me are born refugees; later in my life, I got a chance to change my life, and the US helped me a lot with this desire. The opportunity the state provided to move to a different state helped me take another direction in life and be successful.

After coming to the US, my problems did not end, and I still have them, but I became aware of how I and many of my fellow Bhutanese were exiled. Problems are part of life whether you are rich or poor; we all have to face some challenges to get our work done.

When I moved to New Hampshire, I found several Bhutanese Americans living there and facing many problems; they couldn't even come out of their house and interact with people. Finding employment was another problem for them, and I wanted to help them not because I wanted fame but to give back to my society.

Soon, I came to know some young and educated Bhutanese Americans there; we started talking to each other and discussing the problems of the resettled Bhutanese who were not educated. The common ground between us brought us closer, and this closeness made us make a collective effort to help others.

We started small by helping them find social services, get a driving license, navigate to nearby places, and reach their desired locations. Always remember, your effort never goes to waste, even if you lose. Our work brought Bhutanese refugees to get noticed by the people around us. Locals eventually started calling, asking us about the Bhutanese refugees' struggles and our work.

This people's recognition brought the idea to start a nonprofit organization to help Bhutanese Americans scale up. With the help of some friends, we turned our vision into a reality, but we did not have the funds. Therefore, we had to volunteer along with our full-time jobs and family responsibilities.

Years passed while helping newcomers and managing passion and responsibilities together, and soon we found that some foundations could help us monetarily. Unfortunately, we did not know anything about writing grants and submitting them. Yet, the burning desire enables you to find a solution, and that's what happened in our case. There is no boundary to learning new things; we learned to write and submit grants at different places.

I could remember my experience of submitting at one place; there, the man came outside to receive us, and I handed him the application. Fortunately, we secured a grant of some thousands of dollars. Those dollars helped us run our Bhutanese Community of New Hampshire organization. The money allowed us to support other communities and collaborate with them. At one point, we employed twenty people for different services like mental health, social service, and youth empowerment program. I started as a volunteer; later, I became a full-time staff and executive director for a brief period.

Since we covered numerous communities, we had to change our name to let others come to us, so the community soon turned into the Building Community of New Hampshire. In the beginning, I was one of the organization's founding members, but later I became the executive director and a member of the board of directors before giving my resignation after years of service in 2022.

The organization is quite well-managed. It's heartwarming to know we helped many resettled Bhutanese adjust to the US. In the beginning, there used to be 2100 resettled Bhutanese in New Hampshire, but then many moved to Ohio and Pennsylvania to unite with their family and get better employment opportunities. Currently, around 1500 resettled Bhutanese are there, but there is no official data as people frequently go and come in.

You never need a reason to help others, but your brain needs a reason to become a passionate change-maker. We started with the motive to help our Bhutanese brothers and sisters, and with time, we got another reason; it was to unite them.

Bhutanese society is very divided, both in Nepal and in other countries. We wanted to help them become economically stable enough to support their families in New Hampshire. Once we started our work, many organizations joined us.

So, many Bhutanese nonprofit agencies help our people find jobs, establish small businesses, and engage in profit sectors. Many individuals and successful business owners are willing to help needy organizations and individuals in Bhutan, but the Bhutanese government is unwilling to accept our help. They do not provide us with visas and let us visit the country for a few days and do something great or small for our native land. We want to see our fellow Bhutanese happy and thriving in their way. We want to show our love and support to a country where we opened our eyes.

The community and the ongoing pain and suffering motivated us to bring Bhutanese to the diaspora and the government for discussion to find a win-win solution because we want our people to visit the country and meet their loved ones. We want the political prisoners to be released. We want betterment in Bhutan. Expressing our opinions angrily could not solve the problem; it could be solved when both parties remain calm and come to one ground to discuss the issue.

The current state of resettled Bhutanese makes me happy but also a little sad because many are successful in their lives but still have their roots missing. Some are employed in large companies, many have started their business, and some are going for further studies. However, the goal of returning to the country to meet their loved ones is not achieved, which makes me sad. Yet, the former refugees will make it through because we are resilient; the struggling phase in Nepal has prepared us to face any challenge and walk long miles to get our way.

Therefore, I hope this hard time will pass, just like every other phase in our lives.

Chapter 23

My Opinions

Life is a combination of problems and success. Whether it is a person or a state, problems are the central part of it. After all, it is why we continue to live, experience different things, and learn from what we have faced. When I came to the US, I thought that my life would not be less than a bed of roses, but I was wrong.

I faced more challenges than I ever anticipated, from finances to jobs to education, but fortunately, I honed my skills and prepared myself to face them. Counselors assisted me in understanding the situation while job training sessions prepared me for interviews, and college scholarships made academics less troublesome. Yet, language was the biggest challenge I faced.

Every country has a set of challenges to face. We have an example of Africa, which has been impoverished for over three decades. The problems between Israel and Palestine have been in front of our eyes since childhood. Thus, Bhutan is not alone in the pool of issues. Progress matters and Bhutan is moving ahead, becoming a better place to live as the government is slowly democratizing the country. Yet, seeing my hometown's new air of hope took ages. Nonetheless, the efforts were worth it.

Bhutan was not always against Lhotshampas.

The truth is that it all started in June 1974 when King Jigme Singye Wangchuk was enthroned. In 1952, Bhutan State Congress organized a movement, asking the government for equal representation and democratization.

According to AHURA Bhutan, and other independent writers, he was not responsible for the ethnic cleansing or forceful eviction of Lhotshampas because he was just a teenager when he replaced his dead father.

Prominent international relations experts, including the US Congress and various stakeholders, made a fervent plea to the king of Bhutan, urging them to clearly elucidate the prevailing situation to the monarch, in the hope of enlisting his benevolent intervention to protect the Lhotshampas. Unfortunately, these endeavors yielded no positive outcome, as the head of state exhibited a conspicuous reluctance to endorse measures that would enhance the welfare and security of his people. This was particularly evident in his hesitancy to address the looming ethnic cleansing crisis and ameliorate the ongoing political challenges within the nation.

His father made just rules in the country that promoted growth and diversity. Still, his death aroused opportunities for ministers and misled the king, who had no idea what to do but was not ready to accept others' suggestions, AHURA Bhutan suggests. Teknath Rizal, the advisor to the king, was asked for the suggestion. He advised, consequently, to stop the evictions of Lhotshampas. The new king did not appreciate his advice and tortured and imprisoned him for decades. Later, he was even exiled.

Like the king, the ministers saw Lhotshampas as a threat because of their growing population and interest in political matters and academics.

That's when the government decided to politicize the southern part of Bhutan or the habitat of Lhotshampas. Implementing the Nationality Act, 1977 planted the seed of discrimination and political ostracization. However, it did not become an issue until Bhutan Citizenship Act 1985 was passed. It created chaos in the country as it was considered the first step to evicting Lhotshampas.

The community had to show their identity card or Certificate of Origin (CO) to prove to the authorities that they belonged to Bhutan. The census from 1988 to 1989 became the most significant issue that resulted in protests. Eventually, the demonstrators were beaten and imprisoned by the government authorities.

Although Lhotshampas fought for their rights and democracy, innocent people got trapped between the community and the government. They suffered the most, especially when forced to leave the country or imprisoned just for asking for their nationality and right to practice their culture.

Therefore, I feel that the 1990s was the culmination of the suppression to snatch God-given rights from the people. The illiteracy and long marches worsened the problem because the government had all powers. None could defeat them. Some influential people were on the side of Lhotshampas; however, they could not bring international organizations, as they lacked strategic, social change movements, resources, and foreign support to solve the problem. It was necessary to take a step at that time. One had to sow seeds of human rights and democracy as thousands were exiled and faced brutal punishments. Currently, the younger generation seems distracted from their fight due to the need for survival at hand.

Eventually, in 2008, the Bhutanese government had no viable option to continue its authoritative nature, as the dictators started kneeling before democracy, resulting in a remarkable transition. Although people still complain, their efforts reaped the ripest fruits, and none could deny it. Many who were against democracy then, now hold high-level political positions. Irony.

The 1990s was a time of forceful implementation of their plans; therefore, it was no less than impossible for international organizations to work on Bhutan's issue when there was already an issue with Sudan, Ukraine, Iran, Rwanda, and others.

I remember one letter sent to the former King of Bhutan by the US Congress, asking the King of Bhutan to come to California to attend the conferences and discuss the conflict in the country. So even after the conflict, more than 100,000 Bhutanese were exiled. Some moved to other countries, like me, when they got a chance, and some stayed in Bhutan.

Unfortunately, Lhotshampas are not united to resolve the Bhutan issue. Similarly, there is no unity among political parties. Everybody wanted different things and ideas to be implemented in the country. Yet, the good news is that after the conflict, democracy was introduced in Bhutan, and the head of the government was elected after every five years through general elections. Today, there is a constitution in the country.

Although Bhutan is improving and people consider it peaceful, the issue still lingers. Bhutanese who migrated to other countries could not visit their home country because of their rigid laws and fear. A few years back, I met a lady whose father died of cancer in Bhutan, but she could not see him at his funeral.

Later, her mother died in Bhutan, and she wanted to visit but could not. Lhotshampas are still living there as second-class citizens. They are not happy in a country that vehemently promotes Gross National Happiness. It seems that GNH came to sugarcoat the unhappiness of the people.

Scores of people are still in prison, and many are missing. Bhutanese men married to Indian women do not get citizenship in the country. Their children still have no citizenship rights in Bhutan. Their wives cannot visit Bhutan; they have to pay Rs. 1200 each day to visit their husbands' country. Thousands of Christians live in Bhutan, but still, there are no churches as the government feels threatened by Christianity. They do not get burial space in Bhutan, so they have to cross the border and go to India to bury their loved ones.

They shared their grievances with the king and prime minister, but they still cannot register their Christian organization and right to pray in the nation freely. Therefore, they are not allowed to register any Christian organization because the government thinks that Christianity is against the country's cultural heritage.

In papers and news, Bhutan is considered the happiest country; however, Lhotshampas living there are not content; they have been living in the worst conditions for years. The solution to this problem—to make the country happiest for everyone—should not be an arduous revolution but dialogue: communication.

Communication has a solution to every problem, big or small. The models and principles of peacebuilding and reconciliation could help the two parties, refugees, and the government, understand each other and reach a solution. The goal should not be to win over each other but to resolve the issue and restore peace. Both parties should come out of revenge because revenge does not encourage justice and fuels the cycle of violence. Building peace ends the cycle of violence and leads to reconciliation.

There are many approaches to resolving complex issues. Negotiation, top-down, and bottom-up are a few approaches that are applied in many other countries. This is, in many cases, a short-lived solution. Top-down appears appropriate in this case but undermines the healing, justice, past wrongs, root causes of the conflict, and reconciliation. But this can help find common ground and craft a way to help the oppressed people visit Bhutan to meet their loved ones or address outstanding issues. It involves looking at the problem from the big picture and then working on its components.

In my opinion, meeting the four conditions of the intergroup contact theory can help the parties come up with the solution: equal status, common goals, intergroup cooperation, and support of international authorities.

The government of Bhutan is influential, but refugees need to get united to be as eminent so that both have equal status. Both have to find a common goal that they can discuss in depth. The intent should not be to defeat the other party but to address the injustices and commit to not repeat them in the future. To achieve this goal, no approach is more appropriate than peacebuilding and reconciliation.

In the case of Bhutan, their goal should be to resolve the issue, not to win against each other. The third condition can't be met unless they get support from international organizations.

Fortunately, our efforts have yielded fruits, and people have started talking about the issue of Lhotshampas. Today, some organizations are motivated to solve the matter and help both parties come to dialogue and listen openly without prejudice.

The truth is that no issue can be solved without cooperation; both parties have to make compromises for the betterment of Bhutan.

The concept of peacebuilding and reconciliation has given me hope, and I hope to solve this issue and gift a peace-loving state to refugees in Bhutan. We hope it will help us fix the problem of people living in camps there. Resolving the matter will benefit Bhutanese residing outside the country and boost the tourism industry, improving the state's economy.

Bhutan is a nation of peace-loving people.

My aim for my country is that it would become a pleasant place for its people. Even though I spent my life in the US, my heart still lies in

Bhutan, and I want the best for the country where I grew up. That's why we are trying to bring refugees and the government to one table to realize our dream. And we know it will be fulfilled because nothing is impossible to do when the crowd is united to work on their dreams.

If I am allowed by the government of Bhutan to come to the state, I will choose to return to Bhutan and live there my whole life.